CHUCK, MY WALK THROUGH LIFE

CHUCK

My Walk Through Life

Chuck Woolaver

Copyright © 2016 by Chuck Woolaver.

Library of Congress Control Number:		2016917779
ISBN:	Hardcover	978-1-5245-5432-3
	Softcover	978-1-5245-5431-6
	eBook	978-1-5245-5430-9

All rights reserved. No part of this book may be reproduced or transmitted in any form or by any means, electronic or mechanical, including photocopying, recording, or by any information storage and retrieval system, without permission in writing from the copyright owner.

Any people depicted in stock imagery provided by Thinkstock are models, and such images are being used for illustrative purposes only. Certain stock imagery © Thinkstock.

Print information available on the last page.

Rev. date: 10/26/2016

To order additional copies of this book, contact:
Xlibris
1-888-795-4274
www.Xlibris.com
Orders@Xlibris.com
752043

TABLE OF CONTENTS

Preface vii
Important Items of Note ix
Acknowledgement.. xiii

Chapter 1—What it's all about 1
Chapter 2—My Story Starts Here 2
Chapter 3—Starting at The End 5
Chapter 4—The First Step 7
Chapter 5—Frustration and Awareness 9
Chapter 6—How Bad Is It...12
Chapter 7—The Next Procedure, A Potential Life Saver.........16
Chapter 8—A Second Chance 20
Chapter 9—We Started with The Heart, Now What? 23
Chapter 10—Now to Fix the Artery to the Kidney.................26
Chapter 11—A Leg Up...29
Chapter 12—Wanting to Do Something More........................31
Chapter 13—Know Your Meds 33
Chapter 14—A Respite, Christmas, and My Wonderful Sister...........39
Chapter 15—Two Good Legs...42
Chapter 16—Holy Grapefruit.. 44
Chapter 17—The Early Years 47
Chapter 18—Home Life as A Kid...53
Chapter 19—Off to College...56
Chapter 20—College Daze...58
Chapter 21—Kate and I 62
Chapter 22—A Life Choice...65
Chapter 23—Instant Family 69
Chapter 24—Kicking Around 72
Chapter 25—My Career Path Begins 74
Chapter 26—The Next Chapter, Literally................................76

Chapter 27—A Secure Job…Until 78

Chapter 28—Knuckleheads 80

Chapter 29—The Beginning of the New Beginning.............................84

Chapter 30—2 + 2 = 5..87

Chapter 31—A Change of Plans...89

Chapter 32—So now what?...92

Chapter 33—Philosophy 101 94

Chapter 34—The Aha Moment 95

Chapter 35—Life and Loss..98

Chapter 36—More Philosophy and Stuff...101

Chapter 37—Stop Trying to Keep Up with The Joneses 103

Chapter 38—My "It" 106

Chapter 39—Closing Comments...109

Chapter 40—Closing Comments…Really.......................................111

PREFACE

They say life is like a jigsaw puzzle. There are plenty of pieces. Sometimes we can put the pieces together to form a picture or an outcome, and sometimes it seems like there are a few pieces missing. Mine was pretty much the former until life changed and it abruptly became the latter.

This is a book, written in bite size chapters, that reflects on the pieces in my life, both the good and bad. It is about the twists and turns life can take, but more importantly, how we handle them. It is also about opportunity. We all have opportunities that confront us in life. Sometimes we recognize them, sometimes we don't. Sometimes we realize that an opportunity was staring us smack dab in the face after it is too late. The million-dollar question is: what did we do about it? Did we act? Did we pass? Did we embrace it and throw all caution to the wind and go for the ride of our lives? How did our decisions to act, or not act, form the paths our lives took? What was the ultimate outcome? What could it have been if we had acted differently?

This book speaks about my choices and non-choices, and how my life turned out thus far. It goes a bit further in dissecting a medical condition and the associated impact on my life.

It's meant to be fun, informative, and a bit philosophical. It may evoke thought and reflection. It may even make you get up from the couch and do something you never thought you would do. It could be something big and life changing, or something small and yet very rewarding. It really doesn't matter, as long as it brings you joy and fulfillment. Otherwise, what is the point, right?

Thank you for reading my story, and I would be very interested if somehow, someway, you find your "it" in life, and all the pieces of your puzzle fit together properly. I would enjoy hearing your story.

Chuck Woolaver
cwoolaver@gmail.com
It starts with the heart!

IMPORTANT ITEMS OF NOTE

A portion of the content of this book is about heart disease, which also goes by many other names, including cardiovascular disease and coronary artery disease. Much of the information that is generally available about heart disease can be confusing, as there are so many factors that can lead to this disease. In my opinion, the scientific community still has many questions to answer relating to the actual causes of heart disease.

In the book, I touch on my personal experience with coronary artery disease related to a process called atherosclerosis (plaque build-up on the walls of the arteries). This is my own experience which may or may not be similar to others, however it does offer insight into my battle with this deadly condition.

I am not a doctor, nor should any of this information be a substitute for an opinion or diagnosis of a physician. Anything that can be construed as advice, is simply my own personal opinion. I will always say, check with your own doctor for your own particular situation. Beyond that, I do believe it is important to be your own advocate, or have someone available to advocate on your behalf. The more informed you are, the better the discussions with your physician will be, and eventually the best treatment options will be chosen.

As for Cardiovascular disease, it can come in many forms, including heart valve problems, arrhythmia, heart attack and stroke, and can be caused by many factors. Here are some important statistics to remember about heart disease:

- Heart disease is the number one killer in America
- About 1 in every 4 deaths are related to heart disease

- People of all ages and backgrounds are candidates for heart disease
- Coronary Artery Disease is the most common, accounting for over one half of all heart disease related deaths
- Every year, approximately 735,000 Americans have a heart attack. Amazingly, approximately 210,000 happen with people that have already had a heart attack

Risk factors include:

- High blood pressure
- High cholesterol
- Smoking

Other medical conditions that can put you at risk include:

- Diabetes
- Being overweight or obese
- Poor diet
- Physical inactivity
- Excessive alcohol use

Know the warning signs:

- Chest pain or discomfort. Sometimes confused with heartburn or acid reflux
- Upper body pain or discomfort in the arms, back, neck, jaw, or upper stomach
- Shortness of breath
- Nausea, lightheadedness, or cold sweat

This information was obtained through various sources including the American Heart Association, the Center for Disease Control and Prevention, and The National Center for Health Statistics.

My goal and the goal of our organization, Walk For The Beat, a 501(c)(3) nonprofit, is to create a movement towards living a heart healthy lifestyle. Knowledge is power, and it is my personal belief that many of us put our health into the background as we tackle other challenges in life.

Without a doubt, life can be hectic. We have a tendency to prioritize many other aspects of our lives above taking care of our bodies and our heart. This book talks about the choices we make in life and where those choices may take us. It really is more about some of life's bigger decisions. I will ask, as it relates to your heart health, that no matter what age you are, that you consider some of life's smaller decisions as well. That includes, whether or not to exercise; what you buy at the grocery store; whether or not to start smoking (don't); and how to manage the stress in your life. All of this plays a role in your long term heart health.

Walk For The Beat is attempting to move the heart disease discussion back into the forefront of our minds. It is our belief that for a variety of reasons, that heart disease has lost a bit of our nation's attention.

Our goal is to educate America's youth on the value of exercise and a healthy diet. We will provide life-saving training tips, doing so before, during, and after our walk across America starting on 10-01-2017. There is no limit to what we can achieve.

For more information and to follow our progress, check us out at www. walkforthebeat.org.

Another item of note: You will find out a lot about me reading this book. One thing is that I am not perfect, another is that we are saving our resources for our big adventure. Therefore, I did not pour money into professional editing of this book. It just seemed like an added expense that we could avoid. A luxury of sorts. A few people provided feedback and I read it over a few times. If you find a typo, I apologize in advance. We did our best to make this book grammatically correct. Sometimes we get all caught up in the minor details when the message is really what is important, so please keep that in mind. Thank you for your understanding!

ACKNOWLEDGEMENT

There are so many people to thank for me being able to write this book. Heck, there are so many people to thank for me just being here, when I could have easily become another statistic at age 53.

I will start with the medical staff. To Dr. Kazziha, you know how I feel about you personally, and I cannot begin to describe how awesome you are professionally. Your accomplishments speak for themselves. Thank you for being so good at what you do, and for having a great sense of humor, which believe it or not, helped tremendously.

To our friend and Physician Assistant, Charlene Bailey, your quick response and decisive action may have saved my life. The care you provide to, and show for your patients is exemplary, especially the hugs. Thanks from Kate and I, from the bottom, top, middle, and sides of our hearts.

I have been told that I am a lucky man because my condition was caught in time. I am also lucky to have such wonderful friends and family, all of whom have supported me both emotionally and physically over the past year and a half. There are literally too many to name, but they know who they are, and I will make darn sure they continue to hear how much I love them.

People are not measured by the amount of money they have, or the size of their home, or the type of car they drive, they are measured by the number of people who care about them, so yes, I am a very lucky man.

Finally, to the one that holds our entire family together, my wife Kate, well…I know you know, and I know you don't need or want public acknowledgement, but, well, you know. Enough said. LOL.

Lastly, thanks to those that helped with the book. Gavin, Lisa, Kate, Ryan, and Jude. Your input, suggestions, ideas, they all helped shape this book.

I will end with this quote:

> *"I don't regret things I've done; I regret the things I didn't do when I had the chance."* **Unknown**

Read on for more on that subject. I believe they call that a tease. Now enjoy the book!

This book is dedicated to my best friend,
the one who inspires me
to be a better person.

my wife, Kate.

CHAPTER 1

What it's all about

My name is Chuck, and I have a story to tell. Everybody has a story to tell, right? Well, I hope my story holds your interest, provides a few laughs, maybe a few tears, and something of value that you can use to make life even better. After all, we never stop learning.

What is interesting about life, or I should say how people handle life, is that we tend to move through it allowing external factors, in some cases, to determine our path or outcome. Some people tell me they feel like a slave to their job. Some people are in bad relationships but accept it as the way it should be. Many continue on with the status quo for various reasons, and that status quo is their path.

We are all different in so many ways, and the decisions we make lead us down one path or another, often veering through life midstream and taking us to a particular outcome. This is happening to us virtually every day, whether we are aware of it or not.

In this book, I lay out my life and experiences, the paths that I forged and the paths that I allowed to be forged for me. If the book does nothing else, (oh, there will be a few laughs here and there), I hope it makes you reflect on your path and ask the question, is it the best path for me?

My hope is that one of two things are discovered:

1) You are on the path for you and are happy about your life.
2) After thought and reflection, you decide you would like to alter your path, whatever that might be, big or small, and (here is the important part) do something about it.

Chapter 2

My Story Starts Here

I have been told that my story is a compelling one, and that it should be shared. That is why I am writing this book. I have made a decision based on a life changing event, to go outside the box and change my path. Is it a scary proposition? Absolutely. Does it come without anxiety and uncertainty? Absolutely not. Is it within my comfort zone? Not initially. Could it be the most rewarding thing I have ever done? It would have to top the birth of my son, but it could surely be in the top two.

I am setting a new path that is not about how much money I could sock away, which was part of the path I have been on for years, but rather how I can help others who may be on the same course I was on from a stress and health standpoint. This is unchartered territory for me, but territory that I am eager to explore.

I just celebrated by 55th birthday, and time seems to be moving by faster and faster the older I get. They say the older you get the faster time goes by (not in actuality, it just seems that way). So, no time like the present because when you think about it, nobody really knows exactly how much time we have left to live out our dreams, or accomplish what we want in life. Nobody has an expiration data stamped on their body, although I did see someone with a date tattooed on their body, but I am guessing that has some other relevance.

Sure there are risks in making a career or any type of life change. I realize the grass is not always greener on the other side of the proverbial fence. But I ask, how do you know until you try, and what if you fail? At least you tried. That is something we can hang our hats on, isn't it? When it is all said and done, it comes down to the choices we make in life. That is truly what determines our path, the outcome, and potentially our overall happiness.

I recently read a survey about elderly people who were on their death beds, and they were asked a host of different questions. One question was if they had any regrets in life. As you might guess, nobody said they wish they would have worked more. However, every single one said they regret not taking a chance in life. Doing something that they may have believed they had a passion for. It varied from starting a business, to playing a musical instrument. Some wanted to make more of a difference on this earth, feeling as though they didn't accomplish what they were put here to do. I found that interesting.

What prevented these people from chasing their dream? Was it fear? Fear of risk, fear of loss? Was it that the status quo was a known commodity and within their comfort zone? Probably. It was for me for many years. Or maybe they just didn't find time for whatever it was they missed out of in life. Perhaps they never assigned a priority status to it, one that made it important and urgent.

Yet when these people reached a stage in their lives where reaching for their dream was no longer possible, they had regret. Whatever the reason was for not chasing a dream earlier in their lives, what it boils down to is that they consciously chose not to chase that dream. It was a choice.

On the flipside, there are times where we are hit smack dab in the face with the opportunity to chase a dream. When something major happens in our lives that is impactful, it could be anything really, a loss of a job, a divorce, a loss of a loved one, or a serious medical diagnosis, or a lucky break that opens a door for us, we are faced with choices. Choices that will determine our path and where it takes us.

One choice could be to do nothing, continue on the same course, and take the path of least resistance. Continue on with life and maintain the status quo. Safe, known, predictable.

Another option may be to withdraw. Let it get the best of you. This is probably not an option that anyone would consciously choose, but rather what someone allows to happen by inaction or possibly by denial, accepting it as fate; something that was meant to be. People often refer to "things happen for a reason". I'm not sure I buy into that philosophy. Sure, things happen, but it is what you choose to do from there that creates your "fate".

The third option would be to take an aggressive action. By this I mean, make a change in your life. Become involved, find a purpose, take the issue, or life, head on and make a difference.

I am finally choosing what is behind door number three. Everyone's situation is different and there are many factors that may play into the decisions you make. Age, financial standing and responsibilities, family, physical limitations, and many more. The importance that you place on these factors is what will truly determine what choices you will make in determining your future path in life. For me, the time is right and the conditions are right to flip things upside down and do something I never even considered in my 55 years on this planet.

After my brush with my own mortality, an out of the blue coronary artery disease diagnosis at age 53, the questions I asked myself is, why me? Not in the sense of why did this happen to me, but rather, why am I still here? I had a serious medical diagnosis and the timing of finding the issue, and the subsequent treatment, has allowed me to remain on this earth when many others have not been so lucky. When you survive something like this it makes you think. A lot. You reflect on your life, your own mortality, and even though I have done some pretty good things that would make a lot of people proud, have I really served my purpose? What have I really accomplished? Wow, I sound like one of those people surveyed on their death bed.

But seriously, if something like that has occurred in your life, you probably know what I am talking about. For me I felt unfulfilled (I actually felt this prior to my diagnosis, but kept pushing the idea out of my mind as much as I could, whenever I could).

I thought there was more to life than going to work, coming home, eating, walking the dog, and going to sleep. Sure, I have had my fun in life, but what have I really done that helped the greater good? Here is the big question, if I hadn't been so lucky and wasn't diagnosed in time, and left this earth for the great beyond, would anyone outside my family and close friends care or notice? I wasn't even a footnote in this world. I found that to be a bit unsettling and an overall scary thought.

CHAPTER 3

Starting at The End

Let me first tell you about my medical experience in 2015 and then fill in the blanks from there. I am what most likely can be described as a "regular guy". Going through life for the most part, blessed with a good family and lifelong friends. I have been lucky enough to have a couple of good jobs in my career in business, and I've been described as a good athlete excelling in sports like baseball and golf, both of which have provided me with years of enjoyment. A middle class guy's guy, living the American Dream, normal, happy, healthy, facing few of the proverbial curveballs that life is known to throw on occasion. I was continuing on the status quo path because not only was it easy, but life was pretty good.

Sure, like everyone else on planet earth I have experienced hardships. I lost both of my parents while in my 30's, and consider myself fortunate to have had them for that long. I have lost other family members that we will discuss later on in the book. I lost not one, but two jobs due to both company's financial situation. Truth be told, I lost three jobs including my most recent employment of 13 years, but we will get to that a bit later as well. But all in all, I was fortunate for health, ample money to be comfortable and do some fun things, great friends, and best of all a wonderful family.

OK, here is the medical stuff. In February of 2015 I was diagnosed with peripheral artery disease. Huh? I had never heard of such a thing. This is not a very common diagnosis for a relatively young man of 53 years, a non-smoker and someone who seemed to be in pretty good shape. I was

6'1", 180 pounds, and doctors would look at me as if they have never seen anything like this before. It befuddled all the medical staff I saw at the time and all of the physicians and nurses I have seen since, and let me tell you, there have been plenty. But, as I would say on many occasions, it is what it is, move forward and deal with it.

So what is peripheral artery disease? That was the question my wife Kate and I had, along with, what does it mean long term, and what do we do about it? I remember calling her after the initial diagnosis, and telling her she has a defective husband. Little did I know at that time how defective I was.

We were told the arteries in my legs were blocked and that is what caused the pain I had experienced while walking. My calves, (yes, I have calf muscles, although many of my friends who have seen me in shorts might want to argue that claim), were cramping up after walking a short distance.

CHAPTER 4

The First Step

What to do? Not being a medical professional, aside to what I read on the internet (all true, of course), I followed the course of action prescribed by the vascular surgeon, which was to go to the cath lab at the local hospital, have the surgeon intervene by going into the main artery in the groin on my good leg (honestly neither was very good as I would find out, but the left leg gave me less trouble), fish through (I'm pretty sure that is not a medical term) to where the blockage is in the bad leg, and place a stent in the artery in the right leg. This would then open that artery up for blood flow. Blood then gets to the muscles in the lower leg, brings oxygen, and the muscles no longer cramp.

Excellent. In and out, get it done and move on. Well, it wasn't that simple. When the vascular surgeon enters the artery, he injects dye that can be seen on a monitor. He can then see where the claudication (blockage) has occurred, and where to place the stent to fix the problem. I was awake during the procedure and quite honestly, felt pretty comfortable. There is only a slight amount of pain when they access the artery, but you cannot feel the injection of dye, or the device they use to set the stent in place.

Being alert and listening to the doctor and nurse talk, it was clear that he wouldn't be able to accomplish what they set out to do. The blockage was too severe. 100% blocked in my right iliac artery. In addition to that, he could see that I had an issue with blockage to my left kidney (85%), and blockage forming in my aorta. Evidently I was a mess. Being 100% blocked, he was not comfortable trying to break through the plaque in an effort to open the artery. I guess that is a tricky proposition with associated risks. He also tried to get a kidney doctor on the line to see what should be done with that artery. The kidney doctor was not immediately available. At this particular time, there was no mention about the arteries near the heart. This doctor was a vascular surgeon and not a cardiologist, and I am guessing that the die and imaging was localized to the areas I mentioned above.

Now what? The surgeon went out to talk to my wife, who is somewhat knowledgeable with hospitals, procedures, and medical lingo. She cared for her parents and our sister-in-law Karen, as they battled their illnesses, which included many trips to the hospital consulting with doctors. She also does medical billing as a profession, which is certainly a plus. She is comfortable speaking to doctors and assessing these types of situations with information and logic.

Not this time. This was a bit out of her league. She was somewhat apprehensive when the surgeon approached her, not being sure why he was coming to see her so soon. Her initial thoughts were that something was wrong. He approached her, and explained the situation to her. This occurred just after she had called our son Ryan, who was away at college, to provide an update and joke about what they would do with the life insurance money. She immediately feared it wasn't a joking matter.

The surgeon explained the blockage was too severe to repair with a stent and that he was not certain how to proceed with the blocked kidney artery. He asked what she had thought. Now, it may be standard protocol for a surgeon in this situation to ask such a question, but to this day, Kate wonders what he could have possibly expected her to say. They also explained to me that since I had a slight amount of anesthetic administered to take the edge off, that they could not include me in on this decision making process, as if I would have known what to do.

Regardless, without Kate being able to make a decision, life insurance or not (just kidding, I hope), and me not able to as well, they decided to button me back up. It was kind of left at that, oh except for the 6 hours I had to lay on my back to make sure I didn't bleed out from the access point in the groin artery, and the subsequent allergic reaction to the iodine in the dye, which caused a trip to the ER upon arriving home and noticing most of my body was incredibly itchy and beet red.

CHAPTER 5

Frustration and Awareness

Now what do we do? We felt like we were left hanging a bit. My wife believes the surgeon suggested to see a cardiologist, but couldn't quite remember. Do I go back to my general physician? Kate changed doctors moving from my general practice doctor years ago after a misdiagnosis, and has been bugging me to do the same. Therefore, I saw no reason to go back to my original general practice doctor. Do I schedule a follow up with the vascular surgeon? He did refer me to a nephrologist (kidney). Was that the next course of action? Again, I'm not an expert, but other matters seemed more pressing. Recovering, itchy, and not sure what to do next was perplexing.

This occurred on a Thursday. Kate baby sits two of our six lovely granddaughters on Friday at her son's house (my step-son), and not wanting to leave me home alone, mostly due to the allergic reaction, she took me with her. She probably figured, what is one more baby to watch?

As we sat and talked that day we were confused and frustrated, and my nervousness grew. Ultimately, we determined that blocked arteries in the leg, kidney, and aorta probably means I should have the most important arteries around the heart checked as well as the carotid arteries (stroke). Makes sense, huh? It took us a while to get to that conclusion, but quite honestly I'm not sure the medical people that we were entrusting were going in that direction. At the very least, there were no communications from this medical staff to us on what we should do next. So now that we have that understanding, who do we call? Do we pick a name out of the yellow pages?

I had not followed my wife's advice for years regarding my doctor. Again, she had told me to find a new doctor since her misdiagnosis some 20 years prior. Throughout that time, I thought, I don't need to do that. Nothing is ever wrong with me and he is a nice guy. I go in, get my annual physical, and all is good. Well, now things have changed. We felt I needed someone a bit more proactive.

Kate suggested that I see her doctor who technically isn't a doctor, but rather a physician's assistant (PA). To add a bit of irony, this particular PA had a heart attack about a year prior, so she not only knows the profession, but has first-hand experience relating to a potentially similar heart issue.

Kate proceeded to call her on my behalf. They had worked together at a doctor's office where my wife had once worked, and had built a friendship. Kate asked the million-dollar question, "should he see a cardiologist and start with the heart?" The PA suggested to see her on Monday morning and we would go from there, but she also stated that "YES, chances are good that if there is blockage in the legs and near the kidney, that there is a good chance that there is blockage near the heart." It makes me wonder why the last group of medical people didn't take that path initially, but no need to go backwards here at this point. We wanted to find out what was wrong and fix it. You hear about so many people that had no warnings, that drop dead of a heart attack, and we didn't want to add to that statistic.

It was a bit scary to think I might be a walking heart attack waiting to happen, but I will say that we were relieved that at the very least, we were on the right track. A couple of sleepless nights and what do you know, it is Monday morning and we were in my new doctor's office.

She looked at my bloodwork and said, "wow, your cholesterol is not good." I had an EKG done and if I recall correctly a chest X-Ray. She then said, "I am going to see if I can get you into my cardiologist today, he is right up the road and the only doctor I wanted to work on me when I had my issue."

I found out later that as my new doctor was having her heart attack, she took five baby aspirin and drove herself to a hospital that was quite a bit farther away than the closest one, just so this particular cardiologist could work on her. That was risky as time was of critical importance, but a risk she felt worth taking. I felt that was a pretty good testimonial, and it made me feel more comfortable about our new direction.

He agreed to squeeze me in, and as I have come to find out, that was not such an easy task. He is a very busy man in high demand. I could imagine the conversation they must have had, (PA) "Dr., I have an interesting patient that you need to see today." (Cardiologist) "I am booked solid, and can't see him today." (PA) "Yes, but I guarantee that this one will put your kids through college, he needs a lot of work." (Cardiologist) "What do you know, I just found out I am free at 2." Wouldn't that be funny. I am joking of course but it would make an interesting conversation.

CHAPTER 6

How Bad Is It

So we arrived at the cardiologist's office and waited for quite some time. I am not a fan of waiting, and it is funny how doctors don't like it if you are late. They actually charge you if you don't cancel in time. But, at this time, in this instance, a was being a patient patient.

In time I was called in and had my blood pressure taken. It was a bit elevated which was not normal for me. Then the cardiologist comes in. He is pushing a computer cart and has the results from my blood work.

The first thing he said to me was "wow" when looking at my cholesterol. That was the same expression that the PA had when she saw my cholesterol numbers, he actually used the same word, "wow". I asked if the cholesterol numbers were really that bad. No words were uttered, just a stare suggesting that they were bad. That is when I started to sense he was a no nonsense kind of guy. Quick side note, Kate attended virtually all my doctor appointments with me. That made it so much easier from my perspective. Just to have someone there to chat and joke with, and of course help keep things in perspective helped tremendously.

I am going to sidetrack you here for a minute to hammer home a point that I want to emphasize in this book. Recently, after all the events and procedures of 2015 occurred, my wife found a bloodwork test of mine from 2004. This is from a different doctor than my original family doctor. My LDL, the bad cholesterol, was 196. I know you just said "wow", because that is what I said when I saw it.

Now I'm not sure when they started breaking down cholesterol into good and bad numbers and in turn, figuring out what it all means, but apparently it was before 2004. Otherwise, I don't believe it would have been broken down in this manner on my bloodwork report. One guess what this doctor told me about my cholesterol numbers, and it wasn't, "wow". Give yourself a prize if you said nothing. He never mentioned it to me. Off the chart bad cholesterol numbers and not a peep from the doctor.

The point that needs to be hammered home is that you have to be your own advocate. I get that cholesterol numbers are confusing. Heck, they keep changing what is acceptable in terms of numbers, as well as what you should and shouldn't eat. Do your best to have a basic knowledge, which is better than I had in 2004. Then, when you see a number like 196 for your LDL, you won't need anyone to tell you anything, you will act on that information, as I should have. Don't rely on the doctors to tell you everything or even be right 100% of the time, they are human and have bad days just like the rest of us.

Ok, back to the story. The cardiologist scheduled a handful of tests that would take about a week to complete, culminating with a chemical stress test that Friday. I couldn't walk on the treadmill to perform the standard type of stress test due to the leg cramping, thus the need for the chemical stress test.

For the record, I found the chemical stress test to be quite unpleasant. I should have known it was coming because the nurse explained to me that if it gets too bad to let her know and she could reverse the effects. At the time, I figured, how bad could it be? I didn't think anything of it. I was a tough guy and wouldn't need to tap out. I was wrong.

I can only imagine what an animal feels like when they are euthanized, the feeling that must come over them the seconds before they die. This had to be similar to that feeling. I'm not sure that accurately depicts the feeling I had for this brief moment, but I'm betting it is similar. As they inject the chemical, you feel as if everything is closing in on you from the inside out and you are slowly losing your consciousness.

I am claustrophobic, and this was worse than any physical claustrophobia experience I have had before. I cried "uncle" soon after she started, and she said it was ok, because she got enough data. We had a follow up meeting with the cardiologist the following Monday to discuss the results.

On a side note, the one test I was not looking forward to was the nuclear imaging test. You lie on a table and a very large camera (machine) starts on your left side and scans for a few minutes, moves a bit farther and scans, and continues to the far right side. By that time, this large machine is completely over your body and enclosing you similar to an MRI machine, a claustrophobic's nightmare.

Before they began this test, they do a trial run with the camera in short order and test to see if the camera is properly positioned throughout the test. This means I have to lie there while the camera encompasses my body, right up to near my chin. My only thought was if there was an escape route as it covered my body. Could I slither out to my right, or was it possibly to shimmy down underneath it to the foot of the table? Anyone with claustrophobia knows what I am talking about.

I am proud to say that with a bit of mental fortitude, I won this challenge without incident. Future procedures would be similar in terms of feeling closed in, and I really had no issue with them. Did I beat my phobia? Perhaps in the short term, but I really have not been tested since. Let's just say I won that battle and lived another day.

Monday morning, with the results in hand, the cardiologist said that I failed the stress test and wants me in the cath lab on Wednesday, that he didn't want to wait any longer.

Incidentally, Kate's first husband's father, my second father-in-law, passed away a few days prior, and the funeral was scheduled for that same Wednesday. Upon hearing that the doctor wanted me in the hospital on Wednesday, she uttered "Does it have to be Wednesday? That is my father-in-law's funeral."

Without any delay, in a sort of a dead panned (no pun intended) response, the doctor stated in a matter of fact manner that "we are dealing with the living and want to keep it that way" and left the room. It was clear that time was important and we both got the point.

Another quick side track. My initial diagnosis of blocked arteries happened in February. During a January snowstorm, Kate and I were at my step-son Joe's house one night watching the grand girls, while he and his wife Michelle were out for the evening. It was cold outside. The kind of cold where they tell you to be careful shoveling snow. Negative temperatures with a 20 mile an hour wind, making the wind chill -20 to -30.

My wife, eternally wanting to help the kids, told me to shovel their snow. Being a good guy, I agreed, although rather begrudgingly. Now mind

Chuck, My Walk Through Life

you, I had no idea what kind of shape my arteries were in, and of course nor did Kate.

I shoveled some of the icy driveway, and used a snow blower for the long sidewalk, and the winds were absolutely frigid. The blowing snow made it particularly difficult and of course I was not happy to be out there busting my butt in such lousy conditions. I did understand that I was over 50 and that our local weather man advised against going outside. So here I was, with blocked arteries, in freezing cold temperatures, angry about the whole thing, exerting myself, creating a potentially disastrous outcome. Who knew?

CHAPTER 7

The Next Procedure, A Potential Life Saver

Back to the story. Wednesday morning comes, I am still upright and taking nourishment, and quite honestly in pretty good spirits. Hey, after all I didn't have to go to work that day, although I had my smartphone by my bed and was responding to emails throughout the day. The staff at the hospital was outstanding and I felt very confident that the outcome would be positive. We joked, talked about family and golf, and my brother-in-law John came by to sit with me and Kate. He is that kind of guy.

As it turns out, I am not the first one scheduled for a procedure that day, although we were told to be there at 8 AM, and on top of it, there is a delay. This time I didn't mind the delay as we were having a few laughs in pre-op. So all is good from my standpoint.

Anyways, the man scheduled before me was late arriving due to a problem with transportation, and since they are off schedule, and he is not there, I would be next in. Awesome, now I am ready to get on with this and move forward.

Well, this man arrives before I can go in, and is not happy that he is being bumped, like he is going to miss his connector flight at the airport. Really? C'mon, just lie back relax and watch TV. But he was not having it and was getting a bit unruly.

He called for the doctor; yep, the one who would be performing my procedure, who quite honestly has better things to do than argue with a disgruntled patient. They had a somewhat heated discussion, and the doctor then came to me and apologetically asked if I wouldn't mind waiting a bit longer.

Now, the last thing in the world I want to do, is inconvenience or upset the man that is going to be operating on or near my heart. I emphatically told him that I was fine and that he should do whatever was convenient for him, and that I was just as happy as could be lying in bed, half naked, watching old re-runs of Mayberry RFD. We laughed and he was appreciative.

By now we are a few hours behind and I guess you could say I was getting a bit restless. I wasn't nervous really, just uncomfortable from laying in a bed that I kept sliding down, when the head of the bed was elevated. Plus, I was constantly trying to adjust the gown that was riding high, so to speak.

TV didn't offer anything worth watching, John had to leave for work, (he happens to be a nurse, by the way), and there is only so much Kate and I could talk about. I checked my smartphone now and then to answer any work related questions and probably dozed off a time or two.

Finally, it was my turn on the table. We made a few friends in the staging area as Kate, who has a heart of gold, brought a candy basket for all the wonderful people that worked in that department. She later brought another for the ICU nurses. I guess getting on the nurses' good side is not a bad thing, but really, she does it out of the kindness of her heart, and to sincerely show her appreciation for the difficult and important jobs that nurses do.

This was a different hospital than the one where the vascular surgeon unsuccessfully attempted to unblock the artery in my right leg. That first hospital experience wasn't necessarily a bad one, other than the outcome, but it was amazing how wonderful all the people I had encountered were at this new hospital.

Joking and talking to the folks there helped to put me at ease, as now I am starting to get a bit nervous, and the reality of any type of procedure near my heart brought all kinds of thoughts, none of which were warm and fuzzy. What is he going to find? What if something happens while I am on the table? I've heard stories. What if he determines that he can't do anything, just like the vascular surgeon? It is funny how we can let our minds go where they really don't need to, and I am an expert at it.

The room was bright white, very bright, and they place you on a table that has a very large machine over it. Looking directly up from my position is what appears to be a window. It is really a piece of glass with a light bulb behind it. On the glass is an etching of a nice outdoor scene. I can only imagine that it is there to put the patient's mind at ease. The only problem is that when the surgery starts, the big camera/machine moves to a position to where you can no longer see the window scene. I worked to keep my mind clear and envisioned that scene, among other pleasing scenes in my life, in order to stay positive and keep my mind occupied.

Then the preparation starts, which seemed to take forever. In actuality, it probably was only a few minutes, but when you are anxious, time seems to drag on in a way that only perpetuates more anxiety. Warm blankets were provided which felt great as they kept the room cold enough to store meat. The instruments were aligned and the access site prepared. Every step was explained and of course I had to add in the customary wise cracks that I am known for. I guess it helps ease my own tension.

It was then that my doctor walked in. A quick check to see how I was doing, he calls me Charlie and by the way, is the only one that can get away with it, and then he was all business. It is amazing to see such a skilled cardiologist joke around a bit, then flip the switch and focus entirely on the job at hand. It is understandable, but he was intensely focused, and I figured that was a good thing.

Again, a slight amount of anesthetic, twilight they called it, was administered. I would have to say however that I was completely in tune with what was going on. Probably too much so. This procedure called for entry into the artery in the wrist. This method is better in terms of recovery. The patient can sit up post procedure without fear of bleeding as opposed to accessing the groin artery. In addition, walking and climbing stairs is less problematic for the few days after the procedure where you have to be cautious about inadvertently opening up the access site (bleeding from a main artery).

It was my left wrist, however the doctor stood on my right side. For that reason, I had to lay my left arm across my body and hold it quite still during the 45 minute to 1-hour procedure. That might explain the discomfort I had in that arm for about a month after the procedure. I would wake up in the middle of the night and it felt like someone hit my forearm with a baseball bat. It was severe pain but would only last about five minutes and then would be fine. It was intensely painful, however after that awful 30-day period, the pain stopped and never again reared its ugly head.

Anyways, back to the procedure. This time I actually felt the instrument as it traveled through the artery in the shoulder area. As the doctor then explored the left anterior descending artery (more commonly referred to the widow maker), I could feel pressure or what I would describe as slight discomfort in my chest that I had not felt before. Not to be overly dramatic, but it crossed my mind that I could be having a heart attack.

This was all new to me and I really had little idea as to exactly what the doctor was going to do, or find. Not in traditional Chuck style, I relaxed, calmed my mind, said a prayer and thought that I was in a good place if something were to happen, and that if the worst happened, it was completely out of my control so now is not the time to panic (again, not particularly my style).

The discomfort subsided after what seemed like an hour, it was really only about a minute or so, and then started immediately on the right side of my chest. Like it says on the shampoo bottle, wash and repeat, I said another prayer and relaxed. A few moments later the doctor wrapped up, actually he left that to the people assisting in the procedure. Regardless, he finished his job, placed his hand on my shoulder and said I was a "very lucky man".

He proceeded to tell me that he placed two stents in the "widow maker" artery and that it was 95% blocked. I then realized that I was a ticking time bomb and it hit me that if gone untreated, I could have very easily been another statistic. It wasn't a matter of if, it was a matter of when. I still get teary eyed to this day thinking about it. Again, why me? Why was I lucky enough to have this caught prior to what would have been a catastrophic outcome? I have heard of so many people who passed from a sudden heart attack, without much, if any, warning. This includes seemingly healthy and fit people in their 30's, 40's, and 50's.

Chapter 8

A Second Chance

The nice people rolled me out of the cath lab. One of the nurses who was assigned to me in the staging area was Brian, and he was keeping Kate updated throughout the procedure. He was unbelievably nice and reassuring. He is very good at what he does and we later found out that he has almost enough kids to field a baseball team. That must be where he learned his patience. Either that or he was just happy to get out of the house.

Kate was waiting somewhere on the route to ICU. It's kind of hard to tell exactly where she was when all you can see are ceiling tiles. When I saw her, my emotions took over. In typical Chuck fashion, I cried like a baby. It dawned on me that if things turned out differently, that I may never have seen that beautiful face that I fell in love with 31 years prior, and the realization set in that I could have been another statistic in the not so distant future. It was an emotional experience to say the least.

They rolled me up to my room and aside from being a blubbering idiot for a few minutes, I was pretty upbeat and looking forward to a night of rest. It was late afternoon when I was officially in my room in ICU. I was in ICU primarily for observation. It is standard protocol for someone having the procedure I had and I was happy for the extra insurance.

It wasn't long after, that my son Ryan and step-daughter Kim arrived. Kim was coming up from Knoxville, Tennessee for her grandpa's funeral, yep the one that we missed, and it was awesome to see her. I came into Kim's life when she was 9, or you could say she came into mine when I was 22. Either way, we are both fortunate that our paths crossed. She lost her Dad, Kate's first husband, a year earlier in a motorcycle accident, and I believe I provided a father figure and a stabilizing presence in her formidable years. She provided me with someone to love like my own, and now 4 beautiful granddaughters, that aside from not being blood related, I consider my own (whether they like it or not). I couldn't have asked for more. I will touch on this relationship a bit later.

Anyways, I knew that they were coming and I promised Kate that I wouldn't become emotional again. I seem to have trouble with controlling my emotions: yep, I am a sap; and can honestly say it seems to be getting worse the older I get. Yes, I cry during sad parts of movies and my eyes tear up when listening to certain songs, especially powerful/perfect voices, singing beautiful songs. It's just me and I can't help it no matter how hard I try.

I figured when I saw Ryan I would lose it. He's my boy and that's all that needs to be said. But, somehow I held it together and we had a few laughs. Kim is good for that and Ryan ribs me every chance he gets. Kim told me I looked good considering. I think that was a compliment, and that would be the last time I would hear that compliment for quite a while.

The ribbing Ryan provides is all good natured, and I try my best to give it back to him in good order. They were shocked to hear how serious the situation was, and were happy I was still around (even though Ryan brought up the life insurance policy on a couple of occasions).

They soon left for the night, and Kate did as well. She would stay with me and has on many other occasions, however, that was not permitted in ICU. That was ok with me, sort of, as I was in good hands with the fantastic nurses and I was pretty tired. I soon found out that there wouldn't be much sleeping that night.

There was a lot of activity on the ICU floor/wing, and a lot of sensors beeping throughout the night, both in my room, and adjacent rooms. Additionally, they checked on me every hour on the hour, checking vitals, taking blood, and providing meds.

Other than a few shots here and there that I received in my life (immunizations, vitamin B shots, that sort of thing) I wasn't poked all that much. Quite honestly, I never cared for getting a shot, (who does?) but I was quickly becoming an old pro at it. I was now starting to feel like a human pin cushion. That would only intensify as the year progressed.

The morning came, my wife was back at 8 AM sharp, and I was itching to go home. Technically, I was itching a bit from the iodine in the dye, but this time I was prepped with a couple of meds prior to the procedure that included Benadryl, to help minimize the allergic reaction. It worked for the most part, but I still had some redness and itching. It was nowhere near as bad as the reaction from the first failed procedure in my leg, and I was happy about that. With each subsequent procedure throughout the year the reaction became less and less severe. Regardless, I was able to sit up, had breakfast and was ready to go home.

The nurses, who were all phenomenal, gathered and wished me well as they rolled me out to our car. I think the candy helped win them over along with my charming wit and dashing good looks. That's funny, nobody can look good after all of that, especially me. Hair sticking up and I'm sure I had to smell bad. The gown was a mess and revealed my chicken legs, and I was exhausted. Yep, I'm sure I was a sight to behold.

I will say that I am a pretty good patient. I don't like to fuss much and was as accommodating as I could be. The nurses have tough jobs and I could hear some of the stuff they have to deal with, with other patients. The sound does travel in the hospital with the tile floors and thin walls. If I could make their jobs just a little easier, it would be one way to show how much they are appreciated.

I did get a visit from the person in charge of nursing. Apparently, they like to do what I would refer to as an exit interview. I asked her if they do any special training, or have a philosophy that must be adhered to, and I was surprised at her response. Certainly, an organization in which everyone I came in contact with was pleasant, friendly, and did whatever was needed to make me comfortable, must have some sort of special system in regards to training and/or accountability. Maybe I could learn something and use it at my job. As it turns out, and I heard this from multiple nurses, they all just simply enjoy their jobs. Hmm, not sure I buy that, but ok. How cool is that? I later found out that an overarching philosophy at this hospital is to treat patients as if they were guests in their own home. I can honestly say, that is how I was treated. It was awesome!

Back at home and resting. Kate had everything ready for me from reading material at my bedside, to food prepared. She is truly amazing and watching how she cared for her Mom, Dad, and Sister-in-law, I was lucky to have her as my caregiver. She put a bell by my bed so I could call for her if needed. I tested it a few times much to her chagrin. I still had my sense of humor, or at least I thought so.

CHAPTER 9

We Started with The
Heart, Now What?

After the procedure, all reports are that the heart is healthy and strong, according to my cardiologist. The LAD artery is flowing and the other arteries of the heart are in pretty good shape. That is all great news. Of course now I am on blood thinners for the next year, to make sure no clots occur in the newly placed stents. But I am relieved for the most part and eager to get the kidney and legs fixed. I understand the kidney is a priority but man, I really want to walk without pain and get back to gym to exercise with a purpose.

I get it that the weightlifting is pretty much done for me, at least for a while. My doctor insists that walking would be the best thing for me. He has stated that he is convinced that if people walked regularly, with a purpose, that other exercises such as weightlifting are not necessary. Walk, walk, walk, he said, and hearing him say those words has stuck with me to this day.

It is amazing how fast the muscle you build up in the gym disappears through inactivity. I was feeling pretty good about my new physique acquired by recent work in the gym that I will discuss later, but after a month of inactivity it was pretty much gone. I guess I would have to put that in my past. That's ok, I really am into getting my legs back in business

Chuck, My Walk Through Life

and the cardiologist said he would take a shot at clearing the blockage that the vascular surgeon could not fix. But first the kidney.

In terms of stenting a kidney artery, he said "if we do nothing, you will lose the kidney". He stated that there has been no definitive research on what would occur when you open an 85% blocked artery to the kidney, so with the known being that if nothing were done that I would lose the kidney, it was logical that we stent it and see what happens. It's funny that I frequently use the word "we" in terms of my medical care, like I was the guy doing the work. I guess it is because my doctor made both me and Kate feel like we were part of the process, and I was grateful for that.

Let me sidetrack again for a brief moment and talk about blood thinners. You have to be pretty careful when taking them. You have to watch any other drugs you might be prescribed and any over the counter medications as well, as they may have an adverse reaction (as they say on those annoying TV commercials). You also have to be careful to not cut yourself.

One of the first things that Kate recommended I do was buy an electric razor. I of course listened, although if you are used to one way of shaving, changing isn't necessarily easy.

There were three blood thinner related incidents that deserve mentioning. The big one we will discuss in detail later. The first one was my first dose of the new normal, that is living on blood thinners. It was a simple backyard barbeque, where I was the chef, something that I had done hundreds of times. The grill is on our brick patio that is below our wood deck. From the deck, it is a step up through the door wall and into the house. The door wall sits on a row of bricks like you would see at any doorway of a brick house.

As I was going into the house through the door wall after checking the grill, I scraped my ankle on a brick, hard enough to peel off a layer or two of skin. I didn't think anything of it as I walked to the kitchen to make the salad. The salad prep took all of about 5 minutes when Kate walked in and noticed the blood on the floor and asked what happened. I had no idea until I looked down and saw a significant about of blood dripping from my ankle. Well, that has never happened before, and now I know to keep clear of sharp objects.

The second incident occurred while cleaning debris out of our gutters. I've done it a million times and it needed to be done again. Kate insisted she would do it, but this is a man's job, and she is a girl after all (actually, there is no manly man task that Kate wouldn't attempt, and accomplish for that matter, especially when it comes to yard work). Anyways, I have already lost enough of my manhood not being able to do certain things, so I was bound and determined to clean the gutters. The ladder is lightweight aluminum, the gutters aren't that high up, what could possibly go wrong?

Well, I will tell you. I was about 95% done with the job and getting to the last section. I could see twigs coming up from this last section of gutter. Surely this is what is causing the gutters to back up, similar to my arteries in a weird sort of way. I climbed up four steps on the ladder, I couldn't quite see into the gutter at that point, I then reached into the gutter to grab the twigs. At that moment a morning dove, that I could not see, and had no idea was in there, flew out. Startled, I leaned back and that was all it took. I landed flat on my back from about 4 feet or so off the ground.

We have silver maple trees near that side of the house. If you know anything about those trees, you know that the roots are everywhere. Not knowing how badly I was hurt, I just laid there for a moment, mentally taking inventory. As the brain scanned all parts of my body, I realized I was ok and stood up as Kate and Ryan came running. They heard the thud. Somehow I missed all the roots of those big trees which could have caused some serious problems.

Kate suggested I go to the ER because I may have internal bleeding. My doctor later said the same thing. But when all was said and done, I was fine, lucky, but fine.

CHAPTER 10

Now to Fix the Artery to the Kidney

Back in the cath lab a month later and I was being prepped once again, for a now familiar procedure. They had to access the artery in the groin once again, to get to the kidney. This is my third go around with this type of procedure, so at this point, I am an old pro. I was feeling confident and looking forward to getting fixed. The staff remembers us as the nice people who brought the candy a month prior and of course Kate didn't disappoint this time around as well. I asked if she would add some things that are a bit more nutritious, so she added some granola bars and nuts, things like that.

The procedure was a success. When I got back to the staging area I was still bleeding from the access site. You cannot sit up for 6 hours after the bleeding stops to prevent added blood flow to the site and risk of bleeding, it is a main artery after all. But first, we have to stop the bleeding that persisted while I was lying flat.

A nice nurse was trying to stop the bleeding by applying pressure to the site. She sat next to me and was either nervous, or was just one of those types that can't really sit still. She applied pressure with her index and middle finger but was bouncing her leg up and down while she sat. You have probably seen people like that, the ones who are in perpetual movement.

Well, this wasn't working as I could feel her leg bouncing through her fingers, and she seemed to constantly be moving where she was placing her fingers. Now I am not one to necessarily have a problem with a pretty female doing anything near my groin area, but this was getting a bit annoying. I bit my tongue (again, not Chuck like), but I really didn't want to ruffle any feathers, no matter how frustrated I got.

Eventually she asked for assistance as Mike, another nurse, happened to be passing by. Mike pressed on the site and held still for about 45 minutes. He checked the site every once in a while, to see if it was still bleeding, which by the way, nauseated Kate (we finally found my superwoman's kryptonite).

As Mike was working his magic, we talked golf. He mentioned that he always wanted to play a local private course, Indianwood, that is known as a great links style course and has hosted the Women's and Senior US Opens. As it turns out, I have a connection there and tell him that we will definitely play there once I heal up. I thought that maybe this would be the motivation to fix me up and stop the bleeding. As with all the staff at Crittenton, that motivation wasn't needed. They just do their jobs and do them well.

The bleeding finally stopped and Mike's fingers were locked, he couldn't bend them from pressing them into my artery for so long. I felt bad, but was thankful. I got his name and asked if he was on Facebook. Fast forward, Mike and I connected on Facebook, and my nephew Ned and his boss Brian, my connection to the course, got us on to play Indianwood's Old Course on a beautiful Tuesday morning. By the way, thank you fellas, so much. It meant a lot.

Once the bleeding was under control (I later saw the bed sheets, it wasn't pretty, as there was a lot of blood on them), it was again up to ICU, but this time I believe it was due to room availability and not monitoring the heart or anything like that. Once I was there, my assigned nurse talked about what they were going to do in terms of protocol. This included a shot of heparin. Heparin is a short lived blood thinner, and after bleeding for almost an hour, Kate and I questioned whether or not I should receive that shot. We were told that we could refuse it, and we did. I was already on a blood thinner, I had trouble stopping the bleeding after the procedure, and we determined that refusing the medication was probably best. This is an important point in terms of being your own patient advocate, and we brought it up with my cardiologist at my next visit. He agreed we did the right thing.

What I tell people from this experience is that you have to be your own advocate. You have to ask questions, and you have to have a basic understanding of the course of treatment and why it is needed. We were told it was hospital "protocol" to administer this med to those who had a procedure that I just had. But in my situation, it wasn't needed or, as we felt, appropriate, and could have caused more harm than good.

It was about 3 PM in the afternoon, and they told me to lay flat on my back for six hours. Well, I wasn't about to bleed again and start all over, so I stayed flat until 6 AM the next morning, 15 hours. By the way, the groin area is very tender and having someone push on it for even a few minutes is uncomfortable. I was hopefully done with that process and didn't want to risk having to go through it again.

Somehow, someway, it wasn't an issue lying flat for that long. I typically have restless leg syndrome while lying on my back at home which is why I am a side sleeper. For some reason I didn't have it that night, thank goodness.

Kate arrived the next day bright and early with bagels for the nurses, and we were released and on our way home. The second of four procedures (not counting the initial procedure with the vascular surgeon), is a success. The next step is to see what Dr. Kazziha can do with the 100% blockage in the right iliac artery.

CHAPTER 11

A Leg Up

Back to the hospital a few weeks later and I am now a seasoned veteran. Heck, I could probably do the procedure myself if they would let me, LOL. From not having been in a hospital since I was 9 years old, I was now on my fourth visit within four months, for another important procedure. I have to admit it has taken a toll both physically and mentally. I have lost weight and strength, and have lost a fair amount of desire to give it my all at work. We will touch on that later.

These procedures seem to be relatively simple as far as operations go. By that I mean there are no large incisions, no bones cracked or muscles cut. However, my wife insists that I need to take it easy, as they are somewhat invasive and that I have been through a lot over that past few months. I fought that notion at first, but I was starting to feel drained, and finally I was beginning to agree with her.

The doctor has given me no guarantees as to whether or not he can get through the blockage. He said he will give it a try and if unsuccessful, bypass surgery would most likely be needed. Without blood flow to a leg, there is the possibility of amputation somewhere down the road. Of course I wanted to avoid both amputation and bypass if at all possible. I am still not clear as to the risks of at least trying to break through an artery that is 100% blocked. I assume that damage to the artery could result in internal bleeding (just my own assumption not based on any medical information), but as it turned out, there were no issues and my new favorite doctor did the job placing two stents in my right iliac artery. No bleeding episode occurred with this procedure as they used a device that seals the artery at the access site, and apparently dissolves over time.

After these surgeries you have to take it easy with walking, no lifting of 5 pounds or more for 5 days, and be very careful climbing stairs. The last thing you want to do is start bleeding from a main artery when you are away from the hospital. I was given instructions on what to do if it does start to bleed. Place as much pressure as you can on the site and when you think you are pushing hard enough, push harder and call 911 immediately. This didn't seem to pleasant to me, so I was extremely careful.

I walked a bit more each day and as I was able to walk around our block, which is about a half mile, I was happy to notice that the cramping was gone. Blood and oxygen was getting to my lower leg. It felt great to walk without pain in my right leg.

CHAPTER 12

Wanting to Do Something More

We were now into the summer months and I was back in for a few tests to use as benchmarks. The left leg is also becoming more of a bother and the testing on that leg shows blockage at and below the knee. The pain is in the front of the lower leg similar to the area where you feel shin splints. We decide to put that off until the end of the year. Too much of my golf season has been interrupted and at least I can now walk the course when I play and, carry my bag. Overall, I'm feeling pretty good even though the left leg is hurting a bit.

During one of my office visits with the cardiologist, I mentioned that I want to do something to help the cause and get involved. He had an idea of telling my story on an internal TV commercial, even though I have a face for radio. The discussion didn't go much further and we left it at that. I still felt there was more I could do, but life took over and it remained on my mind, it wasn't high up on the list of priorities at the time.

Summer passed with a lot of golf having been played, and a trip to the Outer Banks with Kate in late September. We love it there and she is especially fond of the east coast, particularly the ocean. Our hope is that we can retire there one day. Then the last trip of the year which was a buddy golf trip to North Myrtle Beach.

On the Myrtle Beach golf trip, I scheduled time with a real estate agent to look at two properties. We were somewhat interested in both. Actually, I was interested in one and Kate was more interested in the other. That is how it always seems to work with us. Regardless, being the man of the house you know who will win that one, right? Yep, she would, if it would have gone that far.

We scheduled to go back in November the weekend of Kate's birthday, and we would take Ryan with us. Flying to Myrtle Beach is relatively inexpensive and we were only going to stay one night at our favorite place, The Avista in North Myrtle Beach. Prices are great during the offseason, so it is a small price to pay to potentially find your retirement home.

CHAPTER 13

Know Your Meds

But first, Halloween rolls around. We love Halloween. We have the perfect neighborhood for it with lots of kids, and our subdivision is in the shape of a big oval. I like to think that we invented putting the fire pit in our driveway for Trick or Treating, but someone probably did that before us.

Halloween was better before they moved back daylight savings time, but again, it is what it is. We also bring out a few beverages with us and many years the kids have roasted hot dogs over the fire.

I like beer, always have, but I have cut back since my diagnosis, trying to limit my beer drinking to a maximum of two when I do drink, and keeping it relatively infrequent. I actually drink a bit of red wine now, which I never did before, with the understanding that red wine provides some benefit to the heart.

Well, I had more than two drinks on Halloween and woke up the next day with a pretty severe hangover. The only thing that ever worked for my headaches was ibuprofen, and I completely forgot to check to see how ibuprofen would react with the blood thinners I was taking. As I had come to find out, the day before we were scheduled to leave for Myrtle Beach, that drinking alcohol, taking ibuprofen, and taking blood thinners was not a good combination.

It is Friday morning the day before we are to leave for Myrtle Beach. My stomach hasn't felt good for past 12 hours or so and the gas I am passing is not normal. It was even getting to me and is not the usual rose-like smell (joking of course). Not to be overly disgusting, but this is somewhat of a medical account so no holds barred, I noticed the toilet was primarily red after my bowel movement. Even I know that is a not good thing.

I do remember the cardiologist saying that if I were to ever experience abnormal bleeding, to immediately call him. Of course, I figured it was a one-time thing and it would be gone by the next bowel movement. I've had hemorrhoids before, and surely that was it. This time the bleeding was due to the hemorrhoids and it was exasperated by the blood thinners, or at least that is what I thought. Nope, not it.

As the day progressed, my gas became worse. Even my wife, who has been known to change the aroma in the room on occasion (salad always gets her), noticed. We laughed, and being the typical guy, I didn't tell her about the morning issue.

Now it is Saturday morning and we are up and packing. Duty calls once again, and there has been no bleeding or bowel movement since Friday morning. I figured I was fine and whatever caused the bleeding on Friday surely has passed.

Sure enough, the toilet is red again. Now I am a bit worried. I tell Kate, and of course being the smart one, she calls the doctor. He tells us to go immediately to the emergency room. Me being the eternal optimist, (well, sometimes), decide that we should take our luggage to the hospital with us. It's 7 AM and our flight doesn't leave until 11:30. I figured that the hospital staff will look at me, tell me to stop the blood thinners for a day, and let me go home. Not so fast, mister.

We explain that we have a flight to catch, and they simply laughed. "Oh, you're not going anywhere today", was said to us by the ER doctor, "other than your room here on the 5th floor". The trip to Myrtle Beach is cancelled and Kate will be spending her birthday in a room other than one overlooking the ocean.

I told her that Rochester, Michigan is nice this time of year (not really), but she wasn't buying it. Our plans to see our future retirement condo was put on hold. Looking back, we felt this may have been fate. Had we bought a condo, we probably wouldn't be planning to do what I am about to tell you, so stay tuned. Sorry about the tease, but you will find out more about fate and what life has planned for us in a bit.

Ok, so losing a bit of blood is not that big of an issue, right? What is really bad is the smell of the gas that is coming from my back side. It is now at DEFCON 5. We are in the hospital room now and the smell is making me gag. All Kate keeps saying is "oh my god" as the gas is being emitted every 10 minutes or so. Then a nice, pretty nurse (somehow all the nurses I met at this particular hospital last year were pretty) walks in and stops dead in her tracks from the odor. I apologize, and she says, "don't apologize, when people have gastrointestinal bleeding, it always smells bad". Still, it was embarrassing. If I were with the guys, it would have been a proud moment, but not in front of my beautiful wife and the pretty nurse. I wasn't fooled by her politeness by the way. The look on her face when she first entered the room and encountered the smell said it all.

The nurse leaves the room in search of an air freshener and comes back with hand sanitizer. That is all she could find. We laughed, tried it, and of course it didn't work. That is when she told me I was scheduled for a colonoscopy to see if they could determine where the bleeding was coming from. I've already lost more weight than I would like and knew this would likely subtract a few more pounds from my already thin body. Before all this happened I weighed about 180 pounds. Now I am 167, primarily from eating better and walking a lot, I guess.

Then, I started to think. Yes, I know, that is not one of my strong suits. But it did dawn on me that if blood is primarily what is coming out my back side, and they give me a laxative, what is going to happen? It can't be good.

This time I was right. It has been a few years since my last colonoscopy and back then I was prescribed some kind of foul tasting laxative. Now they put powder in Gatorade. How about that? Even better, it is the lemon lime kind that I like so much.

She brought in four large Styrofoam cups of the Gatorade and laxative and told me to drink them relatively quickly. They tasted good, so I drank them just about as fast as I could. I later found out that drinking them that fast wasn't a very good idea.

As I thought, the trips to the restroom produced mostly blood, and now my hemoglobin level was becoming dangerously low. There were two doctors consulting on this issue. My cardiologist and a gastrologist. You still have to be concerned with the heart and the relatively newly stented LAD artery. That is why I was still on blood thinners after all, and my cardiologist was not a fan of missing a single blood thinner dose, even if it would only be temporary. He ultimately conceded as we really need to get a handle on the bleeding, otherwise a transfusion would have been required. That is something you want to avoid if at all possible, especially with heart patients.

For the normal person a hemoglobin level at 7.0 or lower would require a transfusion. For a heart patient it is at 8.0. Mine is now being checked regularly and I am ranging between 8.4 and 9.0. I should be around 13.0. If I continue to lose blood, a transfusion would surely be needed. This worried me a bit.

However, I really wasn't thinking about my hemoglobin, as the bathroom continued to call. It was about 3 hours after I drank all that Gatorlax (I just made up that word) and I was starting to feel nauseous. I couldn't tell you the last time I vomited, but I know exactly when it is going to happen. I get this hot flash along with the nausea, and that will do it, which is exactly how I felt. It was becoming clear that I drank that laxative concoction too fast.

It was a good thing that Kate left to go home and get her change of clothes for the evening, as what happened next was not a pretty sight. For the record, this time she would be spending the night. Little did we know it would be the next three nights. See, I can be romantic, a three night stay at a five-star hospital for her birthday. We did have a private room in the new part of the hospital, so all joking aside, I thought the accommodations were excellent, aside from not having an Oceanside suite.

Anyways, I spent the next few minutes alternating between sitting on the toilet and passing blood, and standing and vomiting Gatorlax. It was not a pretty site as one time it happened simultaneously. I had no control. As you can imagine, that particular episode made a mess. It's a good thing I wasn't sharing a room.

It soon passed and I did the best I could to clean the restroom. I stumbled back into bed and felt drained. As bad as that episode was, it was the last of it. I could finally rest and watch the Michigan State – Nebraska football game.

Being a Michigan fan, it is hard to root for Michigan State, even though my friend's son played on the team. I enjoyed watching Nebraska pull off the win. I was after all, still stinging from the Michigan State miracle victory over my beloved Wolverines about two months prior on that now famous botched punt. So, the football game was the highlight of my day.

Kate returned and we slept. At least I did. Kate is not a fan of hotel beds and sheets, so she opted not to use any of the hospital sheets the nurse offered up. She curled up on the vinyl couch which I'm sure was not very comfortable. I shouldn't say I slept all that well either, because I was on a blood drawing schedule every 6 hours to check my hemoglobin, and of course they checked vitals every 2-4 hours. I slept in between the pokings.

The next day was the colonoscopy. They checked my plumbing from below, as is standard with that procedure of course, and put a tube down my throat to take a look from that end. As you probably know, you are completely sedated so I was no worse for the ware. I was starving though. I hadn't eaten since Saturday morning, and now it is Sunday afternoon, and my stomach had to be completely empty.

The results of the tests found nothing, similar to my last brain scan (just kidding). Everything is normal, which is good from that standpoint. They could not see where the bleeding was coming from, and I do have some pretty cool, gross but cool, pictures.

So, no identifiable cause of bleeding, now what? It was determined that I would continue on a liquid diet until my next bowel movement and see if the bleeding stopped. I missed two doses of blood thinners now, so that might help.

Sure enough, Monday morning's bowel movement occurred like clockwork, even though I hadn't eaten in two days. I was however a bit apprehensive about what I would find. What if it was still bleeding? See, there I go again, forever the worrier. But it was much better (I will spare you the color details other than it wasn't red from blood).

I was happy for that, and thought I could eat soon. Again, not so fast. They still wanted to wait awhile to make sure it would remain that way, and there was talk of another colonoscopy, so it was a diet of broth (the beef broth was horrible by the way) and popsicles.

The popsicles were great, even though sugar is something that I have cut out for the most part, and my night nurse brought me as many as I wanted. What an angel. Of course she was pretty too, and sweet, and young. I thought it would be nice to introduce her to my handsome son, however it wasn't her shift when he came to visit.

Later that day they decided against a second colonoscopy, and breakfast the next morning never tasted better, even though I had to order from the heart smart menu. Which deserves mentioning that some of the items on there don't seem heart smart to me, but I wasn't complaining. Anyways, it was different than the doctored up oatmeal I usually eat, and tasted fantastic.

So now I am down to a scant 160 pounds, having lost seven pounds from this episode. We spent that last day in the hospital mainly to make sure my hemoglobin was stabilizing. It had, other than one bad (inaccurate) reading, and I was scheduled for departure the next morning.

That episode took a lot out of me. With a lowered hemoglobin, I was tired. Also, for some reason, laying around in bed for a few days makes you even more tired. You would think it would be the other way around.

This episode took its toll in more ways than just the weight loss. I found it difficult to walk around our half mile block. I soon found out it would get better each day, and much to my surprise, my new general physician (PA) prescribed a steak dinner for me. She said this would help raise my hemoglobin. I don't eat steak much anymore and sometimes crave it. This particular steak was delicious.

She also prescribed iron pills but I found that they gave me a pretty bad headache. I don't function well with a headache so I stopped taking them and haven't had a problem with bleeding or my hemoglobin since.

CHAPTER 14

A Respite, Christmas, and My Wonderful Sister

Next it was down to Tennessee for Thanksgiving. I was tired and a bit frail, but enjoyed the time with Kim and Vahan, her husband, and their four girls. They are a lot of fun. Miriam the oldest, turned 16 recently, accommodated her poor Papa by agreeing to play quite a few games of chess with me. I enjoyed it, and I believe she did too. It was nice to unwind and enjoy the family.

Knoxville is nice. The winters down there are far less severe than Michigan's obviously, so we were able to get in a round of golf. It is a highlight for me to be able to do that after the golf season comes to an end here in Michigan.

One more procedure on the left leg was all that remained. We scheduled it for late December which in retrospect was a mistake, however my little sister Alice, who lives near San Diego, California and who was diagnosed with breast cancer recently, was about to undergo treatments after the first of the year. We had to go see her, right? Alice and I enjoyed many holidays together when we were kids, and we haven't been able to get together like this for a very long time. It is too bad it has to happen while we are both battling illness, but again, we had a choice, to go or stay home. We made the right choice.

My son Ryan and I decided to travel out to spend Christmas with Alice, her daughter Ymani, and my older sister Anita and her awesome family. Anita married an extremely nice guy, Ben, and our family is very lucky for that. They have a cool son, Sam, who is 11 or 12, (I lose track), and looks like a younger Ryan. So much so that people do double takes and wonder if they are brothers.

Ryan and I flew to Las Vegas, it was cheaper, and drove to Los Angeles, where Anita, Ben, and Sam live. Alice and Ymani would meet us there for the holiday. Ryan had never been to Vegas and wanted to see what it was all about. I am not a gambler, but I had been there before and like the architecture, the people watching, and the action. We picked up our convertible, we soon found out that it was too cold to drive with the top down, but tried it anyways. We spent one night in Vegas, drove to LA, and enjoyed a fantastic Christmas with love, drink, great food, fun and a few tears.

Looking back now, Alice and I, who again spent many Christmases together as kids, say this was the best one yet. No stress, no issues, a trip to the beach the day after Christmas, and we had a really good time. We both realized, that with our respected issues, that it is possible that one or two spots at the dinner table could have been vacant. We tried not to dwell on that and remained optimistic that we are going to be survivors and are here for a reason (another tease, sorry).

Alice is a good natured person with a great sense of humor. She is a single mom and has done a tremendous job raising a sweet and loving daughter. She is full of life, and although the cancer diagnosis is scary, she is on the right path with treatment. She does have the protein (HER2) which promotes the growth of cancer cells, but post chemo results so far are pretty good. We are staying positive for the both of us and trying to enjoy life to the fullest. No bad days!

Alice, Anita, and I 2015 Holiday

CHAPTER 15

Two Good Legs

We are now back from Vegas. Ryan and I flew home, and a day later we were back in the hospital for the final procedure on December 29th. I can't tell you how much I am looking forward to having two good legs. To be able to walk without pain, to walk greater distances and speeds, to walk up hills without having to stop, this will make it all worthwhile. This procedure will clear out whatever blockage that there was in my left leg. Simple, been there done that, it should be a breeze. Again, not so fast.

Everything seemed same old same old. Of course by now we are well known in the pre-op area, even though none of the faces are familiar. I guess our reputation preceded us. Kate had the candy basket prepared, and we were once again treated extremely well.

I was back on the table and ready to get this over with. A few jokes with the staff and in came the doc. He cracked a joke and went right to work. I don't think he knew what he was in for. As it turns out, my left leg is blocked behind the knee, and he can't place a stent there, and below the knee in multiple places down to the ankle. This time I felt it.

It was a lengthy procedure taking about 2 hours. Normally, these procedures take about 45 minutes, even the heart procedure took far less time. I'm still not sure exactly all the work he did. He mentioned ballooning behind the knee, placing a stent further down below the knee, and ballooning even beyond that. I still have some swelling above my ankle from the procedure, which is easy to see on my boney legs. I think it is there for good.

It is customary that when the doctor finishes, that he would go out and explain the procedure to Kate, as well as draw a picture of where he placed the stents. I think he feels he is a good artist. Of course being such a lengthy procedure she began to worry, not her style, but her mind was put at ease by Brian, who was giving her frequent updates. The doctor, explained the work he did to Kate and said, "I even impressed myself with this one". He mentioned that most likely, at some point in the future, I would need surgery on that leg.

Now a doctor being impressed by his work is probably not all that uncommon. Even for my doctor, the self- proclaimed "plumber". He once told me that he has a pretty big ego. Hey, if he is saving lives and giving folks like me their quality of life back, he can have as big of an ego as he wants in my opinion.

On a side note, it was during a check-up appointment after the heart procedure, that we brought him a card with a restaurant gift certificate, as if that is enough thanks for possibly saving my life, and a red "Mr. Incredible" t-shirt. He always wore red tennis shoes in the office. It was a perfect match and probably fed into his ego a bit, but that's ok.

He immediately laughed and I figured he had no idea who Mr. Incredible was, so I attempted to explain. He quickly cut me off and said, still laughing, "I know who he is, but didn't he get fat?" We all laughed and I found it funny that such a busy and skilled cardiologist knew the details of The Incredibles movie. He then proudly showed the entire office staff, and their response was something like, and I am paraphrasing, "oh sure, just what he needs".

The last procedure occurred at the end of the year, on December 29th. This allowed for us to get it in on the calendar year where I obviously met my out of pocket max. Sounded like good planning, right? Well as I said quite a few times already, not so fast.

I was discharged, but found out soon that there would be a complication. The device that stops the bleeding when they seal up the artery, leaked. I noticed a red line below the skin that started at the artery above my groin and proceeded down to my right testicle. Sorry, but I have to explain this one just as it happened; it seemed like every healthcare professional in the county would soon be familiar with my now inflamed testicle.

CHAPTER 16

Holy Grapefruit

The testicle was a purple color and about twice the size of the left one. We watched it for a couple days and it didn't get better. It was actually becoming worse and I was in severe pain in about every possible position. Sitting, standing, lying, you name it, it hurt. Lying flat on my back provided the most comfort, as long as I had on loose fitting shorts. Again, sorry for the image.

The weekend passed, and I went into work for a meeting the following Tuesday. I couldn't stand or sit for too long and was in obvious pain. Gary, the guy I was meeting with, finally told me to go home. He was understanding, as most men would be, and we both knew that this had to be worse than childbirth. Just kidding, ladies. It didn't take me long to heed Gary's advice and I drove the hour it takes to get home from the office, in severe pain. Once home, I immediately went to lie in bed for relief.

A few hours later Kate was home and I wasn't able to find that relief. Another observation of the testicle and I determined it was time to go to the emergency room. Yep, now it is after the first of the year so there is a new deductible and co-pay. But, it had to be done and I was not looking forward to it.

Back in the hospital for the 7th time in less than a year, the ER nurse gave me morphine. I never had that drug before, and I was surprised at how fast it worked. I was relaxed and the pain had lessened almost immediately. That feeling didn't last long however, and I didn't request any more medication even though it worked. I'm not a fan of taking pain medication if I can do without.

Now the fun starts, a parade of people of all medical disciplines came to look at my testicle. Most of them touched it for some reason or another, even the female doctors and nurses. If there was any shred of pride left in me from all my visits to the hospital, it surely was now gone.

They decided to do an ultrasound on my testicle and that sounded horrific to me. Surprisingly it wasn't. Of course, the ultrasound technician was another pretty, young lady and my pride was now delving into negative territory. She was training another girl and they were both very nice. I told her I was sorry that she had to work on my, well you know, and she responded, "why?" I guess it is no big deal to these professionals and just part of the job.

The next day, another doctor, a urologist came to visit, and of course needed to see and touch my swollen testicle, except he did a more extensive investigation. He had the results from the ultrasound and determined the bleed took place near a canal that led into the testicle (my luck), and that I would be fine. They would observe me for another day, which meant another overnight and this room didn't accommodate Kate staying. I missed that, but for some reason I don't think she did.

One thing the urologist did do that provided some relief was to fill a pillow case with some type of padding and had me elevate my testicle. Who knew? Not sure why I didn't think to try that earlier, but then again, I never heard of anyone elevating a testicle. A sprained ankle, tendinitis, swollen feet, yes; a testicle, nope.

The next day my favorite cardiologist and a team of interns, (Crittenton is a training hospital for med students from Wayne State University in Detroit), came and he immediately said, "ok, let's see it", in a way that made me feel like it was pictured on the 11 o'clock news. I responded with my usual sarcastic wit "well, everyone else in Oakland County has seen it, you might as well have a look too." He initially didn't think it was a bleed from the procedure site, but I think I knew better this time. Who is the smart one now? Ha! Regardless, he took the urologist's word for it and that was that.

So now, after four successful procedures and one not so successful, the heart arteries are clear(ish), the kidney is clear and performing as it should, and my legs feel pretty darn good. Not perfect but good.

He would later explain that there are other ancillary arteries that he would not be able to fix, but continued to tell me to walk. "Walk, walk, walk" were his instructions. In doing so, the body in its usual amazing fashion, would heal itself. The arteries will actually create their own bypasses in time. So I am taking his advice and walking as much as I can. More on that later.

CHAPTER 17

The Early Years

I'd like to provide you some information that led up to this point in my life, so let's go right back to where it all started, the beginning. After all, part of this story is about what makes us who we are, what paths we choose, the subsequent result, and how the pieces of our individual puzzle begin to fit together. Your childhood plays an important role in it all, or at least that's what the TV talk show psychiatrists tell us.

I was born in Detroit on October 1st, 1961; yep, the same day that Roger Maris eclipsed Babe Ruth's single season home run record with his 61st home run. That was my claim to fame, being a huge baseball fan as a kid. It's not much, but hey, nobody else I knew could make that claim.

We moved from Detroit to Warren, a suburb of Detroit, the summer of 1965 just after my sister Alice was born. Detroit was becoming more and more dangerous, as this was the prelude to the riots of 1967, that are still etched in my memory.

The house on Desmond Street in Warren provided a perfect place for a kid to grow up, or at least get older. A lot of us friends from the neighborhood insist we still haven't grown up, and every now and then we prove that theory. There were a lot of boys around my age and it turned out that we would spend the vast majority of nearly every day together.

I met my first real friend that summer just prior to turning 5. Gavin, who lived two doors down and whose house had to be the very first official Kool-Aid house. They had a backyard that was perfect for baseball with a home run fence that only a titanic blast could carry. I think we once measured it to be 95 feet. They also had a perfect brick fireplace where we placed tape for a strike zone, and had epic games of strikeout. The yard also served double duty, as we played football and a bit of soccer there in the fall.

Gavin's mom never disappointed. She catered to our every whim, letting us sleep over, feeding us, taking us to baseball card shows and to the local ice cream shop. She was my second mom for sure. A sweet, wonderful, caring lady; oh, and patient too. I'm sure we tested that patience from time to time with the worn out base paths on the grass, and the ongoing repetitive thumping of a ball against that fireplace. She never complained.

As we got older, the field no longer could contain our prodigious home run power. It was about that time that Charlie and his family moved in on the hill behind Gavin's house. They moved from a nearby neighborhood and did a tremendous job fixing up the old house. It was on a couple of acres and had a bigger baseball field with a white picket fence (the new home run fence). The home run fence was cool, except I am sure Charlie's dad was not fond of the fact that many a hit ball would break the top off the some of the pickets. Over time, the fence resembled a kid missing half of their baby teeth.

I knew Charlie prior to him moving into our neighborhood, because he was in my grade at Bever Elementary. Truth be told, we weren't all that fond of each other. He was a cub scout and wore that hat with the small brim, that I made fun of every chance I could get. Of course he reciprocated by making fun of the baseball hat that was permanently affixed to my head. We would trade barbs from time to time, but now we were neighbors and we decided to shake hands and figured that we would have more fun if we were friends. It worked out great.

Charlie's mom was about as accommodating as Gavin's. Driving all over the place to go to games and do this or that. It was a blast growing up and between me, Gavin, Pat, Charlie, Scott, Brian, Brett, Alan, two Daves, Ed, Mike, and soon my little sister Alice (who turned out to be a heck of an athlete), we had enough kids to play any sport and field competitive teams. Over the years, more kids would join in from other areas of the surrounding neighborhoods.

It didn't matter what the sport was, we played it. Of course there weren't video games back then and Pong became very boring after a while. Gavin, always the creative one, figured out how to coordinate an Olympic style event which included multiple tests of skill. We played ping pong, ran

Chuck, My Walk Through Life

around the block, lifted weights, threw the shot put (or something similar). Anyways, it was always a competition and was always a blast.

One summer Gavin picked up a Strat-o-Matic game. This is a board game that simulates baseball pretty well by using dice and player cards. Based on their statistics from a respective season, the probabilities of them hitting a single, double, triple, home run, walking, or making an out were pretty accurate. We played it all summer and Gavin, the true accountant, kept track of all the statistics. I guess that was the 70's version of video games because it caused our moms on more than one occasion to say "will you boys go out and play!"

Soon enough the fun would subside. Gavin's dad had been given an opportunity to run a car dealership in Ohio and they moved. I was 13 at the time and was devastated. It was the end of an era. They had a moving sale and we bought a couple of pieces of furniture that they had in their house. These items were a keepsake to me as Gavin's home was my home away from home, even if it was only two houses away.

They were gone but not forgotten, and we made a few trips back and forth to visit. One time Gavin's dad was able to get World Series tickets. Yankees vs. Reds. It wasn't my beloved Tigers but heck, it was the World Series and that was pretty darn cool.

Soon enough we were able to drive, and that opened up a whole new realm of possibilities. I had been moving my dad's car from the driveway so I could shoot hoops, for quite some time, so I was an expert at driving. He let me pull it out from under the basketball net in the driveway and park it by the curb about 20 feet away. What could go wrong? I was 13 or 14 and had driven the hi-lo at his shop. Piece of cake. I, of course, abused this privilege and would often take the car for joy rides. We won't get into the details of that indiscretion, but let's say I found it to be quite fun, and when it came time for my first drivers test to get my license, the instructor said "you are an excellent driver, you must have practiced a lot." Little did he know I have been practicing for 3 years.

Anyways, with Gavin gone, Scott, Brian, and Todd were hanging with us more and sports were no longer really the thing. They still were for me, but most of the others were now into cars, girls, and just hanging out. The court in front of Gavin's old house typically had 5 or 6 cars in it at any one time. The cars belonged to us neighborhood kids and a few from outside the neighborhood that found it cool to hang out with us. It was the place to be and I'm not sure how our parents put up with all the commotion.

We did get into a bit of trouble here and there but nobody got hurt. I mean, every kid lights a street on fire, right? Yep, we did that and were chased. I was petrified.

We were sleeping out one night, in tents and in Charlie's tree house, and someone, not sure who, had the brilliant idea of spraying some lighter fluid across Chicago Road and putting a lit match to it. Chicago Road is a secondary street, but pretty well traveled; and who is on the roads at 3 AM? The cops, that's who.

Fortunately, we could run fast and run I did. Through Charlie's yard and past my parent's big redwood fence. I made it to the garage and hid there, for about two seconds before my mom came out and yelled at me. "Get in this house" she hollered, and of course eager to get away from the cops, I didn't argue, and quickly went in without a peep or objection.

To this day, I still can't figure out how, at three in the morning, and me being as quiet as a church mouse, she knew I was in the garage. Mothers, right? They just seem to know.

It wasn't our first run-in with the police. A couple of years earlier, while Gavin still lived in the neighborhood, he and I decided one night to throw snowballs at cars passing by. Now granted, I would severely reprimand my kid for doing that today, but remember, it was the 70's, the age of innocence, LOL. A great place to perform this incredibly fun but dangerous task was at Charlie's house, right on Chicago Road. They had a pine tree on each side of the driveway and that white picket home run fence bordering the shoulder of the road. A perfect place to hide, with close the proximity to the road, and an excellent escape route if chased.

Of course we turned it into a competition. Gavin and I turned everything we did into a competition. He is a year and a half older than me, so he is usually had the upper hand in terms of winning, but I think he appreciated that I could give him a bit of a battle now and then and make it fun for both of us. Regardless, I always respected his athletic talents, academic skills, and his character as a person. He taught me a lot when I was young, particularly about dedication and discipline. After all, he would read World War II novels into the wee hours of the night. I mean, what 12-year-old kid does that? Anyways, with the competition on, there is surely no way two skilled little league pitchers could miss the cars passing by with a couple of well-timed snowball throws.

We didn't. Bam, bam, first car, two hits, perfect, until the lights and siren on the squad car turned on. In the dark of the night we had no clue that it was a police car. We ran up the driveway and jumped the fence at our friend Dave's house. It was about 8 houses down from Gavin's and 10 from mine, and really, a totally separate neighborhood from Charlie's because of the fences and the hill. We casually walked home from there and said our goodbyes for the night never breaking stride. As I looked back behind Gavin's house and to Charlie's house on the hill, I could see the police shining their spotlights all over Charlie's house. I initially thought that we would surely be busted, but then quickly figured that there are no fingerprints on snowballs.

That's really about it in terms of being mischievous. I really didn't give my parents too much to worry about. They never knew about my underage driving, or for that matter the fire we set or the police cars we hit with snowballs. I received good grades in school up until 10th grade. Then with Gavin no longer around, the report card competition we had between Charlie, Gavin and I was gone and I started to slack off with my studies. See, competition is a driver, it surely was for me.

The poor grades continued through 11th grade, until a school counselor told me I wasn't college material. Now granted, I wasn't in jeopardy of failing to graduate, but I wasn't getting A's and B's that I had been getting up until 10th grade. That one statement from that counselor motivated me to take college prep classes my senior year and ace them all, which I did without too much difficulty. I knew I had it in me to be a good student, I just had to work harder.

The high school years were pretty uneventful, filled with sports and my new girlfriend Kathy. We spent a lot of time together. Charlie hung out with us as he took a shining to Kathy's younger sister Rose. All in all, no stress, no trauma, just a peaceful existence in preparing for the years ahead.

By graduation time however, due to my carelessness in 10th and 11th grade, my grade point average fell below what my dream college, The University of Michigan, would accept, and I had a few conversations with people who were talking about the benefits of going to a small school.

One of those benefits was the ability to participate in college athletics. I'm pretty sure I wasn't good enough to make the U of M baseball team, but I would have a shot at making the team at a small school. Additionally, there was more interaction between professors and students, all of which appealed to me. That and not having to take buses and or ride bikes through the snow 10 miles to get to class, uphill both ways, of course.

I was in a serious relationship at the time, as serious of a relationship that 17-year-old can be in, and decided to go away to school and leave my first love behind. She and I stayed together during my college years, on and off, but we both found other interests. We were young. My interests included spending weekends with my new college friends doing all sorts of fun and stupid things.

The neighborhood guys 1976

CHAPTER 18

Home Life as A Kid

A quick diversion and we will move on to the college years. I don't like talking about it, and 40 some years later, there really is no point. But the early years at home were not all that pleasant. Most everyone has their crosses to bear, and of course, I have mine as well.

There was a significant amount of turmoil in my house. My father worked a lot of hours and my mother, best I could figure, was an unfulfilled stay at home mom. That's how things were in the late 60's and into the mid 70's. They were both loving parents in their own ways, but there were fights, and some real doozies. Fights that an 8-year old boy shouldn't witness, not to mention a 5-year old little sister.

I found myself getting upset at what I witnessed and as I grew up a bit, found it necessary to protect my litter sister by removing her from the fray. That was a big responsibility for a young boy, but I thought it was important at the time. Without getting into too many details, and quite honestly I don't think I ever found out the reasons for all the fighting, the trouble eventually stopped.

Was the damage done? Probably, but sitting here at age 55, I refuse to let that issue define me. Did it create insecurities or other emotional challenges for me? Probably, but someone smarter than me would have to figure that out. Nonetheless, using excuses is not my thing (except on the golf course, LOL).

It was soon after that my mother turned to drinking. She was by definition a full-fledged alcoholic. Why she drank was a mystery to me.

53

Maybe it was the fact that she was getting up in years and had some of her own demons that she could not shake. I hated the fact that she would be drunk whether it be morning, afternoon, or night, and I was always trying to figure out if she was or wasn't. There were multiple times where it would be obvious to a friend of mine who would be over for a visit, and in a couple of instances, very embarrassing.

She hid her bottles, mostly vodka I believe, and I would often search for them and pour them out when I found them. This lasted for a few years and I was between the ages of 12-15 years old during this phase. To her credit, and I don't know how she kicked the habit, but she did. I may have been too young to know, but I am guessing there wasn't a lot of assistance regarding substance or alcohol abuse in the early 70's. I am pretty sure she quit drinking on her own. As much as I hated that this happened, I look back and feel bad that my mother went through this phase.

One day it stopped and that is all that mattered. My mother was a very smart woman. She could fill out a crossword puzzle in no time, and excelled at trivia. My feeling is that she possessed a lot of this talent, and really never utilized it in any fulfilling way. Regardless, although the demons would arise from time to time in fits of anger or rants, she would prove that she cared about us every day, and once the drinking stopped, would be a very loving and caring mother.

My dad on the other hand was for the most part unflappable. He kept a pretty good outlook and was a dedicated worker putting in at least 60 hours a week at his tool and die shop. He wasn't there as much for us as kids from a physical standpoint, but he did provide for the family and was a genuinely loving father.

He would do anything for his kids and that would only become more apparent the older he became. My mother predeceased my father. She was 73 and passed in 1996. My father lived until he was 85 and he died in 2001.

I hesitated to add this information into the book, but it really does mold you as a person and I thought it was relevant information to get an understanding of my life and how my path was forged. It is a piece of the puzzle of my life after all. That includes the good, the bad, and the ugly, and all three have played roles at one time or another in my life.

It comes down to whether or not any of these factors are going to forge your path for you, and do so in a negative way. Don't let them. Again, people smarter than me would have to tell you how to not let life's "crap" forge your path. I just say, don't let it. Simple right? Maybe not. One thing

I can share that helped me, is to never feel sorry for yourself. Never say "oh woe is me". I think this helps provide the mental fortitude to pull yourself up by the boot straps and strive for better no matter what is attempting to drag you down.

Not the best form

CHAPTER 19

Off to College

Soon it was time to start my college career. I left for school one late August morning for orientation. Olivet College was the choice, and with earning a 4.0 my senior year of high school, my application for enrollment was approved. It was about two and a half hours drive time from home, so really, it wasn't all that far. Still, it seemed like a big step to me.

It was an early Saturday morning and both my Mom and Dad were home, which was unusual due to my dad's work schedule. But he stayed home to see me off. My little sister was there too, and aside from all the good natured teasing I gave her over the years, and all the times we annoyed each other, it was a sad goodbye (even though it wasn't really that far away). With a tear in my eye, I drove off to start the next chapter in my life. I remember this moment vividly to this day.

I had to be at school at noon for freshman orientation. Even though I knew it was a small school, I was surprised to find out how few people were there upon arriving at the campus. None of the upper classmen were there of course, and it dawned on me that many of the freshmen were skipping this event.

Olivet was a small school in a small town. The only traffic light in town always blinked. Come to think of it, I'm not sure why they even needed that light. The campus itself was like one that you would see in movies or read about. It was kind of like an Ivy League school in terms of appearance. There were a lot of red brick buildings with a city block common area in the middle of the campus, where many huge oak trees grew. It was particularly appealing in late summer and early fall before the leaves fell.

Anyways, when that freshman orientation event was finished, I went to my dorm room not knowing a single person on campus. My roommate was a Sophomore, so he wasn't expected until early the following week. So I sat in my cinderblock rectangular room, first time away from home, and wondered, why am I here? I walked around campus which took all of about 3 minutes and had something to eat. I read all the materials they gave me at orientation as well as a couple of local restaurant menus and decided that I was already homesick. So what else was there to do but go back home, which I did.

My parents were surprised to see me, but I explained the situation and they seemed to understand. With my little sister still at home for at least three more years, they wouldn't be empty nesters for a while, so they probably didn't care too much that I came back home so quickly.

I hung out with my girlfriend Kathy that evening and then got to sleep in my own bed in my own room one more night, which was more of a bonus than I could imagine when comparing my bed to what I was about to sleep on at school. I'm still not sure how they call it a bed, the concrete floors of the dorm were softer.

It was late Sunday evening before setting sail for school, again, getting the most out of the day Sunday at home. It was a boring ride for the most part and one that I would get plenty used to. They called Olivet College the "suitcase" college. It's in the middle of the state, sort of, and thus it wasn't too far from where most of the students called home, and most importantly, there was virtually nothing to do in the small town of Olivet. Therefore, many students went home on the weekends, leaving the campus desolate except for the die hards that liked to hang around and party.

I looked forward to the week ahead, meeting people and getting acclimated to college life, oh, and the classes too. I registered for classes on Monday, bought my books, and attended a meeting for the golf team. Still no sign of my roommate. I found out that he was the starting quarterback on the football team. That seemed pretty cool.

CHAPTER 20

College Daze

In my first class, I met who would become a lifelong friend, Chris. He was from Grosse Pointe, not too far from Warren, and we would spend a lot of weekends together, both on campus and back home. We also both had an affinity for basketball, so we would frequently go to the gym, which happened to be right next to our dorm. Chris and I were in good shape, and we would go play full court 1-1 basketball late at night when the gym was empty. Seemed like good exercise at the time. Now, looking back, maybe we were both a little crazy.

Sometime later that week, my roommate Bob showed up. Being a sophomore, he had figured out the best way to arrange classes to extend the weekend. There was one problem, he put in for a single, which meant he wasn't expecting a roommate. He was nice about it but asked if I would see if there was another room I could move to. I checked and there was one room that turned out I would have to share with a smoker, who smoked in the room. That was allowed back then and of course would not fly with me.

I declined to move and Bob and I made the best of it. We turned out to be good friends and would do many things together. Our suitemates were also on the football team, both were sophomores and offensive lineman, very large people. Neither were overly intimidating however, and as a matter of fact, one was nicknamed Squeak. They were as friendly and welcoming as could be.

There are a million stories I could share from college. We were knuckleheads for the most part. I'll be brief in giving you an overview of college life while still painting a picture that provides understanding into the minds of said knuckleheads.

Dorm life was never boring, even in Olivet. I was lucky enough to be in the newer dorm that had three floors, new carpet, paint, etc. The rooms were also bigger. The new carpet was similar to indoor outdoor carpeting and was perfect for putting contests, which occurred quite regularly. We had some elaborate holes. This lasted for quite some time until we figured actually playing golf in the hallways was a better idea. This included clubs other than a putter.

The first indoor golfing accident occurred during my sophomore year when someone thought it was a good idea to hit a regulation golf ball down the long straight hallway with a 3 iron. A 3 iron doesn't have a lot of loft, but the ball would get airborne. We would stand at one end and see who could fly it the farthest before it touched ground; at least that was the idea.

The very first shot consisted of a smooth backswing and solid contact. Actually, contact would be made three times, once with the ball, the second time with a door jam on the right about 15 feet from the golfer, and lastly with the golfer's forehead. Said golfer went down and was knocked out as if he was hit by a heavyweight champion's right hook. The ball left dimple marks on my friend's forehead. He turned out to be ok thank goodness.

After that situation, we determined that hitting 3 irons was a bad idea, smart guys, huh? Not so fast, we evolved into hitting wedges. More loft, higher shots, so the ball won't travel as fast. The problem here was that not everyone was adept at golf and the attempted wedge shots would take divots out of the carpeting. These divots were pretty much everywhere, as replacing a carpeting divot is not as easy as a grass divot. It doesn't grow back or stay where you put it.

At about this time, many of the guys in the dorm were of drinking age and of course beer was the popular drink of choice. One of our friends, who lived across the hall, drank bottled beer one weekend and left his door open. The couch faced away from the door to the hallway and towards the TV, which back then in Olivet got one channel and it was always fuzzy. As he finished each beer he would toss the empty bottle behind him, out the door, and they would smash into the cinderblock wall on the other side of the hallway. My guess is that he drank five or six beers and the glass from the broken bottles was everywhere.

When the rest of us got back from whatever we were doing, which I am assuming was playing some type of sport, we noticed the place

Chuck, My Walk Through Life

looked terrible. Divots in the carpeting, broken glass everywhere. We began talking and some genius said it was like a red light district. Now granted, none of us had ever been to a "red light district", but we all had the same interpretation.

So what better way was there to make it an official red light district, then to paint the plastic light covers in the hallway red? A two-dollar investment in red spray paint and we were in business. We were proud of our new hallway. Our signature was all over it. Now we officially lived in the "red light district" of Olivet, Michigan. The mean streets (or halls) of Olivet. We were tough. LOL.

Needless to say, this quickly landed us in hot water. A cleaning crew came in as they did every Monday and immediately went to report this information to the Dean of the college. Of course we denied everything and admitted nothing (see, I did learn something from debate class). That didn't fly of course, and all of us that lived at on that floor, at that end of the dorm, received a bill in the mail for repairs. As you could probably could imagine, the bill for the dorm repairs was a tough one to explain to our parents.

There are countless stories I could tell you about our days at Olivet College. For the most part it was a good school and looking back, it was four of the best years of my life. However, this part of my life is where one of my biggest regrets lies. I was a decent student with a "B" average. But I didn't apply myself as I should have, and I really didn't know what I wanted to study. Sure I did ok in life from an earnings standpoint, but I always thought I could do better. I didn't really have a career that I loved, even though I had the opportunity to put myself in a position to do just that. I graduated with a bachelor's degree in business administration from a liberal arts school. I have found that this is not the foundation for cementing yourself into a specific career path, and that was evident the first 5-10 years post college.

What I should have done is figure out exactly what I wanted to do, work harder than I did, and follow up my four-year degree with two more years and earn my master's degree. That is evident to me now, but it wasn't then for one reason or another.

This of course, partly determined my life's path. I had a degree, so it opened some doors, and I did alright for myself during my career. But in looking back, it wasn't my dream job or what I feel I was meant to do. In other words, I didn't give myself the chance for the right doors to open at that time.

We will discuss how the impact of a choice in life determines your path throughout this book. There is one thing to think about however, (we will discuss it in another chapter; it's a pretty deep concept in my particular situation); had I gone to school for two more years, chances are extremely good that I never would have met my wife. Not meeting my wife would mean my family, kids and all, would not exist as I know them today. Would I be willing to make that change right here, right now? Of course not. It is just interesting to think about it in that light. Stay tuned for more on that topic in a bit.

CHAPTER 21

Kate and I

I am blessed to have a fantastic wife, one that I can call my soulmate. It wasn't always that way, but we persevered and ended up in a truly fantastic place. When I met my wife, she was recently widowed and had two young children. She was 28 at the time. I fell in love with all three of them rather quickly and the rest, as they say, is history.

My step-children and I have a wonderful relationship. We became both family and friends. I couldn't have asked for more or gone back in time and changed anything in that regard. Between the two, Kim and Joe, they have six children of their own now, all girls. They all affectionately call me Pupa. It is truly awesome!

My wife Kate and I met at work, Highland Appliance. She worked in the office, and I had worked in sales there the summer prior while still in college. Once I graduated, not knowing what I wanted to be when I grew up, I went back to work at Highland for a brief time.

We all got to know each other pretty well at Highland. We spent 12 hours a day there and most of our off-time together as well, at one gathering or another. It was a very close-knit group of people even as some came and went, via transfers to other stores, or simply moving to a new job outside of Highland.

I soon found out who Katie was and her story. One thing you will learn about me is that I have a big heart. It doesn't matter who or what it is, heck, I have a hard time killing bugs. Life is important to me and I have a soft spot for anyone who is struggling, and Kate, Kim, and Joe had recently experienced the loss of a husband and father.

Without really knowing Kate all that well. I think up until then we maybe said two words to each other, which probably happened when I needed an invoice to write up a sale. We would have to ask for an invoice from the office staff, that way they could keep track of them. Back then, we didn't have point of sale systems. Many of you youngsters probably didn't know that business still went on prior to computers.

I was walking through the stock room when I overheard Katie say to another girl, who was telling her she should date and someday get remarried, "nobody will ever want to marry me now. I am a widow, I have two kids and…". I cut her off and without slowing my stride, turned my head and said, "I will marry you." I really was just kidding, really.

It wasn't long after that interaction that our paths crossed more frequently. I noticed how pretty she was of course, and how genuinely nice she could be. She often brought in candy for employees and customers, she just did things like that, not much unlike how she took care of the nurses during my hospital visits.

Soon it was time for the annual formal company meeting. Dinner and all, and most everyone brought a date or spouse. I honestly can't remember if I did. One of Kate's friends and I went out on a few dates before I really knew Kate, and there was another pretty girl who worked part time on our store that I had flirted with, but if I recall correctly, I was dateless. Kate, however, had a date to this particular event. Someone she had just started seeing.

Our flirtation that night consisted of trading meals. I have since found out how picky of an eater Kate could be. Whatever she had, probably chicken, she wouldn't eat, and whatever I had, probably steak, she would. It was discussed and the deal was made. I did sense that she wanted it to happen and that she found me irresistible. Of course that is what I thought, but the truth was probably something far less. That was pretty much the extent of our flirtation, although I would catch her glancing at me from time to time. I learned quickly in college when a girl was interested in me, and could sense this was the case. But my shyness prevailed and we left it at that.

A few weeks later, and back at work, and in need of an invoice for a decent size sale, Kate happened to be the one handing out invoices. I asked for one and her reply was "only if you take me out on a date." Aha, she was

63

interested, I knew it. Or was she just teasing me? She was no longer seeing the guy she brought to the annual dinner party, so perhaps there was hope.

Pleasantly surprised and too shy to ask her out, I teased her for a bit and told her I had to see if the commission was worth making the date commitment. That was a joke of course, I was beaming on the inside.

I nervously called her as promised a couple of days later. We decided, my choice actually, to have a drink and see a movie, albeit a bad one in her opinion. I have yet to live that down. It wasn't long after that we spent all our free time together and the relationship was being built. It also wasn't long after that when I began having second thoughts. I mean, I was a young man, only 22 years old, and I was staring a life with a lady and two kids squarely in the eye.

Chapter 22

A Life Choice

Sitting at her house one day, I kept thinking that this wasn't the plan for me. Yes, I loved her and as importantly, yes, I loved her two children, but it just wasn't right. I felt something was out of sorts. Life now was completely different. College was over and I don't see my friends from school anymore. My best friend Mike was still back at school, he was a year behind me. I also don't interact with my friends from my old neighborhood as everyone has moved on with their lives, and here I sit at an unfamiliar place in what I would describe as a strange situation.

It was strange because this was somebody else's family until his untimely death at 28 years old. It was his house, his friends, his wife, his kids, and I wasn't sure that was what I wanted. Yes, my wife is 6 years older than me, and I have gotten a lot of mileage out of that over the years, but that wasn't a factor as to how I felt. Was I supposed to just step in and everything would be normal? It wasn't. Are other people, her friends, her family, his family accepting of me? Would they make it difficult? It was a bit uncomfortable and I explained it to her as nice as I could and she seemed to understand. We both cried as I packed up my stuff and we continued to talk, which would be the foundation of our relationship.

As we talked and talked and talked, I could only think how selfish it would be to leave. I thought about Kate's kids, Kim and Joe and how they needed a father figure, someone to play catch with or help with homework. Up until that time, the kids and I were also building a relationship, and how could I just leave? I couldn't, and didn't, and I have been paid back ten-fold for that decision. Of course, I also knew that I loved Kate, as that goes without saying, however, I really struggled with putting it all in perspective at the time. These are the types of decisions that carve out your path in life.

What if I did leave? My life today would have been completely different, that is if I would still be alive. Who knows? But the choice was made and here I am, with my wife, our family, our kids and grandkids, and I couldn't imagine it being any different.

Kate recently told me about a movie she watched where a guy was able go back in time and change a particular event from the past. He quickly realized though, that by changing this past event, that when he returned to current day life, that the change would alter the future and that things would not be the same as they were before he went back in time.

We had a deep philosophical conversation about this over a couple of beers recently, and she asked me what if anything I would change if I could go back in time. My answer was that I would pay more attention to my studies and most likely followed my father's advice in terms of becoming a doctor.

Her answer to that question was not surprising, she would save her first husband Ralph. There wasn't anything more to it other than how do you not choose to save a loved one's life, especially someone at the young age of 28? I didn't take any offense to it as I understood the logic. I never really questioned whether she loved me or her first husband more. I mean, there really is no point to that kind of thinking. I did however, dream from time to time that he was back and she had to choose one of us. Silly how our subconscious minds work, isn't it? In the dreams, I would always step aside as I figured it would be the right thing to do. Good thing they are just dreams. I don't put too much stock into dreams as I remember that my 12th grade psychology teacher said that things you dream really have no meaning in life. See, I paid attention in school in 12th grade, just not 10th and 11th grade.

As Kate and I talked about this decision of hers to save her first husband, we realized what it would have meant. No Kate and Chuck. No Ryan, which was what she ultimately told me would be the biggest loss. I questioned that of course, and we laughed. Her defense was that she meant me and Ryan…sure she did. Nice try. I did take it a step farther when I realized that I hired our daughter Kim at one of the companies I worked for, as a phone receptionist. It was there that she met her future husband,

Vahan. Now saving Ralph would mean no Chuck, no Ryan, no Vahan, and no granddaughters as we know them. She forgot about that piece of the equation. This was an amazing epiphany and plays into the theme of this book about how the paths in life are shaped, both within and outside of our control.

Those early years, 1984 and on, turned out to be quite fun. Not just because the Tigers won the world series that year, but I would become more acclimated with Kate's fantastic family, and a group of her close friends, many of which would become my close friends.

We didn't make a ton of money back then, not much at all when you think about what it takes to provide for a family of four, but we also didn't miss out on doing many of the fun things in life. Family trips to the lake, the kids sporting events and concerts, family holiday gatherings. It was fun and we had three families, including Kate's ex-husband's family to share the fun times with.

We were married in 1988 in preparation to have our own child together. As wonderful as having Kim and Joe as my step-children was, there was a desire to have one of my own and provide my parents with a grandchild to love. I loved Kim and Joe, but Kate would tell me many times, that having your own child was different. I'm not sure how she would know that, but it was. As much as I cared for Kim and Joe, it was different. Maybe because I was raising Ryan from a baby and had to provide for his every need (still do, he is now 24, just kidding, kind of). Maybe because Kim and Joe would be older by the time Ryan came along. Regardless, both having step-kids and your own kid are great and it has been to this day.

Having our own baby took a while for reasons unknown, and we changed our minds a time or two, but eventually Ryan came along in 1992 to complete the family.

What is odd, is that it now seems like we had two different lives. The one before Ryan, and the one after. Part of it could be because I was still working at Highland Appliance when Ryan was born, and a year later they shut down. I would find new employment and begin a new career path when Ryan was only a year and a half old.

Part of it was that Kim and Joe were now growing up and getting ready to move on with their soon to be adult lives. Things were definitely in the process of changing. As the years went by, Kate and I had our own issues that neither of us are proud of. Ryan was about as challenging as any baby could be and we were both sleep deprived, and stressed.

Other things would lead to our discontent and we both were admittedly guilty of poor judgements or choices. Again, these are the choices that would determine who you are and where you are going to go in life. As bad as things would get, divorce being discussed on multiple occasions, we always found a way to stay together and work through the issues. This "ultimate choice" is what put us where we are today.

Chapter 23

Instant Family

Kim and Joe were 9 and 6 years old respectively when we entered each other's lives. They were about a year removed from losing their father. At first glance, you wouldn't necessarily know that one of their life's puzzle pieces was missing, a big one. They appeared happy, as Kate and her family and friends did a phenomenal job in attempting to move on with life as the new normal.

They were good kids and relatively quiet. I'm sure they were trying to figure it all out and wondered who this guy is that had just entered their lives. I wasn't smart enough to understand what they were going through and how they felt exactly. Heck, at 22 years old, I wasn't sure what I was going through. But I did understand their loss and knew they deserved someone or something that could help fill the void, even it is just a partial fit.

One of my first memories was throwing a Nerf football with Joey in the front yard. Hey, I was still kind of a kid, so why not go out and play catch. Joey had a permanent grin on his face during the catch session. I can still see that smile today, in my mind's eye. It was obvious he enjoyed sports and more than obvious that he was a good athlete. Of course that was near and dear to my heart. He caught just about everything I threw to him which is unusual for a 6-year old. I'm not sure, but I think I won some points that day.

As the years would go on, Joey would be active in little league baseball. Kate and I were able to manage a team and Joey was one of the stars. It was a fun time and something we would share as a family.

There were also school functions like concerts and award programs. Joey was in the Math Olympics although he did fall asleep at the award ceremony. They were onstage and the row that he was sitting in got up to file over to the podium to get their award. Of course we videotaped everything back then, and wondered why a few kids got up and then there was this big gap. In scrolling to the end of the gap, you could see Joey sitting in his seat, fast asleep, while other kids were attempted to wake him up. A proud moment, LOL. We all got a kick out of it.

It was similar with Kim. We gave her a lot of help with homework projects, of which Kate and I took great pride in getting good grades on, I mean, *Kim* getting good grades on. She ran track in high school, and although there were nights where she would weep and say how much she missed her father, she adjusted rather well and was a good student.

When you think about it, Kim and I were only 13 years apart. We had a bit of fun with that. One time Kim, Kate, and I were in the checkout lane in a fruit market and of course I was teasing and having fun with Kim when the clerk looked at Kate and said, "aren't brothers and sisters funny". Of course Kate didn't find this amusing, but I sure did. It must have been my baby face.

The highlight of my relationship with Kim was the honor of walking her down the aisle at her wedding. I never tried to replace their father, but always looked at it as if he was lending me the role of dad, since he couldn't be there himself. This honor was particularly rewarding, even though the nerves were taking over. Due to being nervous, we walked down the aisle at a very fast pace. This was of course until we looked up and saw Kate motioning to slow down. Oops.

At the reception, I also danced with Kim in the customary father-daughter dance. She picked the Celine Dion song "Because You Loved Me". I cried like a baby during the dance and still get teary eyed when I think of it.

Now that they are grown and have kids of their own, it is easy to see that we did a good job in loving, providing for, and raising Kim and Joe. Sure, they had endured tremendous hardship. Hardship that could really affect a child, that could lead to all kinds of challenges in life. But they have both grown to be great people, great spouses, and great parents. I'm not taking credit for that as Kate is a tremendous mother, always nurturing and teaching. Everything she did or said seemed to have a purpose. I like to feel that my presence, perhaps even in a very small way, provided a sense of security and normalness in an otherwise abnormal situation. I will add that it was one of the most fulfilling experiences in my life, one that is still providing me with joy and happiness to this day. This is one of the puzzle pieces of my life that has fit perfectly.

Proud moment with Kim

Chapter 24

Kicking Around

I elected to pursue a career in business after graduating college in 1983. My father owned a tool and die shop and with the unstable economy at the time, particularly in the auto industry (I guess not much has changed over the years), he advised against following in his footsteps. I don't think I was built for that type of work anyways. I was never all that handy and couldn't for the life of me read a blueprint.

I received a Bachelor's degree in Business Administration from Olivet College with a marketing concentration. It was a liberal arts school as I said before, so therefore I know a little bit about a lot of things but not a whole lot about anything. I was not the best student as previously explained, doing enough to get by with a few A's, but mostly B's and C's, much to the chagrin of my father. But then again, I had priorities. Golf in the fall, baseball and tennis in the spring, and then of course there were parties that had to be attended.

After graduating and deciding that furthering my education wasn't really for me, I stumbled around trying to figure out what it was I could do as a career. As with many people I have met in my life it seems like the default job, when you do not have a real specialty, is sales.

I exhibited leadership qualities in some of my sporting endeavors, but was not the most outgoing person around. Kind of one of those guys that had a fair amount of friends but really mostly just fit in as one of the guys.

Sales may have been a stretch for me, being somewhat reserved and all, but then again, without focusing on anything particular in college, there really wasn't anything else that fit at the time. Besides, the money was better than a few other jobs that were available to me.

CHAPTER 25

My Career Path Begins

I would pick back up at the appliance store where I worked summers while in college. I soon determined that wasn't for me. I was there long enough to meet Kate, but felt it wasn't the type of job I would want to do the rest of my life. Certainly, there had to be something that better fit my interests.

I initially started in financial services. I studied for and earned the licensing needed to sell mutual funds and insurance. The stock market and investing in general was a bit of a passion for me, but it didn't take long to determine that I was not comfortable at all asking other people for money. I mean really, I'm 22 years old, fresh out of college, what do I really know about investing, and what if I lose someone's nest egg. I didn't like that idea, and that particular job only lasted a few weeks.

From there I applied for and landed a job as an Assistant Golf Professional at a local course. Sounds impressive, but really all I did was give lessons from morning to night. Back then there weren't many fancy courses around with cool pro shops, and careers in the golf industry were limited. The job turned out to be a seasonal summer job and it was time once again to look for real employment.

I went back to the default job with Highland Appliance. It was not where I really wanted to be, but my friends were there and I didn't have much luck figuring out what else I could do at the time. Retail provided me with long hours, limited upward mobility, and it was certainly not prestigious. With limited options and decent income potential at the time, I was back.

It was December of 1986 when I dove back into the retail pool. I was now living with Kate and her two kids. I had bumped along for the past two years since meeting her, not providing much financial help, but we survived. I stayed in the appliance business for 6 plus years, getting promoted a couple of times, and aside from the crazy hours, looking back, enjoyed my time there. I will say this, it prepared me as a salesperson and as a leader.

The company expanded into markets where the economy subsequently floundered and it cost them dearly. Eventually, they filed bankruptcy and chose to close their doors forever. I worked the going out of business sale and was the last one to lock up the store that I had managed. It was sad, there were many good people there that were out of a job, but as for me it eventually led to bigger and better things.

Chapter 26

The Next Chapter, Literally

Now it is 1993. With a family of five and an infant to care for, I was out on the street, unemployed. It took about six months to find a job. I eventually landed a sales manager job at a local cell phone reseller. It was a small business compared to the appliance company, but had about 200 employees and a solid business plan, along with a significant customer base. We were a blend of retail and business to business sales. My training from the last job provided me with the tools to excel in the wireless retail business. I learned the B2B part on the fly.

The company was expanding, thus the need to hire a manager, and while my store was being built I shared an office with another sales manager for a few months. We made it work.

The wireless industry was taking off, believe it or not, there were still people without cell phones. We also took business from the carriers who sold airtime to us, which we called conversions. These were people that already had phones. We got paid to take them from a carrier and put them on our billing platform. Crazy, but we offered some advantages by being a little more nimble and personal, as well as offering some value added services, such as vehicle installation and the ability to offer both carriers (at the time there were only two cell phone carriers per region).

For the most part the job went well. It wasn't long before I was promoted overseeing all of our sales and sales training efforts. We had 4 physical locations and a team of about 40 outside salespeople. We had all the hierarchy and departments of a large company along with our own billing department. It was very impressive how they built this organization and attacked the big players in the market, Cellular One and Ameritech at the time. There were a lot of good people doing some fantastic work.

I don't have to explain to many folks what happened in the late 90's and how the wireless landscape changed. Legislation opened up the playing field and we saw other companies build, acquire, and/or piece together companies that owned and operated their own independent networks. This occurrence really put the squeeze to the businesses operating on the reseller model, particularly us.

As attrition occurred within our company, I took on more responsibility and wore a lot of hats. It broadened my horizons and added to my experience in business and as a leader. It wasn't long however that the attrition, due to cost cutting measures, affected me.

It was 2003 when I was told that they couldn't afford me any longer and the owner offered me a position in another company of his. It didn't take long to find out that I wasn't a fit and that the pay was not nearly what I was used to making.

I latched on with a dealer (an independent company authorized to sell for a carrier), who knew of me and my abilities. He wanted to expand his outside salesforce and I helped them for about 9 months. The pay was ok, the working conditions were good and the people were nice, but I was trying to do consulting work as well in order to scratch out a living, and it was difficult.

CHAPTER 27

A Secure Job…Until

Through my relationships, I heard of a sales manager position that was open with one of the big five carriers at the time, Nextel. I interviewed poorly with the Director of Sales but my reputation as a solid sales maker and leader preceded me. I was fortunate for that and earned a shot to interview with the Vice President. I did much better in that interview and secured the job.

Now working for a company with 20,000 employees I was about to be indoctrinated into corporate America. I learned to love it and hate it at times. I learned a lot during my 13 years there. Survived a merger (Sprint), won a lot of awards, trips, and made a pretty good living. It was more than a job and for most of the time there felt like a career where I could grow, sharpen the saw, and impact the lives of others trying to do the same thing. Helping others achieve their goals was the most rewarding part for me.

One of the challenges with corporate America is that you really don't control your own destiny. People get promoted at times because they play the game, manage up well, or have a better relationship with a senior leader. I was promoted twice during my tenure there for what I believe to be my own merit, but I think I missed the boat on larger promotions due to other external factors, and partly my own unwillingness to "play the game".

Regardless, after nine years with the wireless reseller, and 13 years with a major carrier, I had built a pretty good resume and felt relatively secure in my career. Something seemed to change however. You can call it burn out, you can point to some overwhelming challenges our company faced, or you could say I was getting into my 50's, had recent health issues that left me with less than the desired energy to do that job. Along with that, was the realization that I was put on this earth to do more than just manipulate spreadsheets and sell wireless technology. It was probably a combination of all of these factors that led to my displeasure with my current career standing.

Stress and frustration crept in on a pretty regular basis. Over the course of the past 4-5 years, the company went through significant organizational changes, multiple times. I had six bosses during that timeframe. Many were moved out, company's decision, or elected to take a severance package as they were reducing headcount. Based on my performance over the years and solid reputation as a leader, I survived all but the most recent "reductions". But with the passion pretty much gone, it was clear that it was my time to go in 2016. Let's just say I saw the writing on the wall.

Let's rewind a year or so and throw in the most important piece to this puzzle. It really is not about a job or a career. It is not about the company you work for. It is about what you believe you should be doing and where your passion lies. Your "it", the thing that excites you and makes you tick. This is where my life changing moment comes in, not welcomed per se, but unavoidable and it slammed into me like a ton of bricks. It is also about beginning with the end in mind and wanted to have as few regrets in my life as possible, as I take my last breaths. We will touch on that more in a bit.

CHAPTER 28

Knuckleheads

This is kind of a diversion from the timeline and career discussion of the previous chapter, but I want to discuss a very important topic. Lifelong friends and my buddies, The Knuckleheads. It goes with my history and is part of my path in life, so I figured I would insert this chapter right here and now. It also ties in with what we are going to discuss in upcoming chapters. So, although it may seem out of place at the moment, I felt it really was a good spot to insert this information.

One of the most comforting things in life is to have lifelong friends. These are people you meet when you are kid, the younger the better in terms of true friendship. You end up knowing just about everything about each other, and as the years' progress, whether you stay close or not, there is a bond that is undeniable.

In my case, I told you about my first friend, Gavin. We grew apart, primarily by distance, as his family moved away when we were teenagers, and of course other interests in life tend to keep you busy. This happened to other friends as well, as many of us went to different colleges and basically lost contact with each other.

The cool thing about a lifelong friend, especially when you grew up together, is that you know virtually everything about that person. You know their birthday, their parents and family, their passions, flaws, fears, likes and dislikes, like I said, virtually everything. You also know that these friends are the ones that will always have your back.

As I have said, our neighborhood in Warren, Michigan back in the late 60's and throughout the 70's, consisted of many kids that were all around the same age. A handful of us are still close today some 50 years later. One thing that keeps us close is golf.

We affectionately call ourselves Knuckleheads and hold an annual golf trip to northern Michigan over a long weekend every August, The Knucklehead Open. I have lost track, but I believe we have been doing this for 20 years. Gavin has travelled up from Texas, where he now lives, and others have joined in as well over the years. We have also travelled to Las Vegas and Myrtle Beach a couple of years to change things up. As silly as it may sound, this trip is a key to our ongoing bond as friends.

One thing to note, and although we have done some dumb things in our youth, and maybe some dumb things recently as well, is that all said Knuckleheads have done pretty well for themselves. Gavin has excelled in finance with his intelligence and work ethic. Scott has made a good living selling cars, utilizing his charming personality and providing exceptional customer service. Scott's brother Brian has done well in the IT and technology world. Greg owns a successful business, and Todd has had a successful career in the automotive supplier world, which is prevalent in the Detroit area.

With that said, all Knuckleheads have gone through a bevy of life's challenges. It seems that nobody can avoid them. I really don't know of anyone that has led such a charmed life, whereas everything from cradle to grave was perfect. Do you? But as a group, we have dealt with our challenges and were always there to support each other.

Some of these challenges include disease, such as coronary artery disease in my case. Todd has battled throat cancer his whole life starting when he was a kid, and today lives with a tracheostomy tube. Mental health issues affected some, while all of us have had to deal with the loss of a loved one. Of course job loss has occurred with most of us, but overall as we approach our latter years, I would say we have all done ok. It really doesn't matter who you are or how much money you have, life is challenging.

As I look as my friends lives in the terms as I have discussed with mine, life's choices and paths, I'm sure there have been regrets. Of course, as Johnny Mathis has once said, "it is not for me to say", but I am pretty sure, based on what I know about them, that each person would have done something differently in their lives.

One of my friends lost a son to a heroin overdose. He has frequently lamented that maybe there was something he could have done differently, even though in my mind he had tried everything and put his heart and soul into helping his son. This included tough love and true love. It included financial support and fatherly guidance. Could something been done to avoid this tragedy? Perhaps, but how can anyone know exactly what that might have been at that moment in time? We do what we can and what we think is best. I know he was a loving father and provided everything you would expect from a good partent. Still, my friend may never escape the feeling that he could have done something, whatever it may have been, different that could have changed things.

Some may regret not taking a particular chance in life, whether it be starting a business or taking some type of risk. Many of us have had conversations about not liking what we do for a living. The truth is that business has changed, and requires more of you. Now that we are in our mid to late 50's, it is really affecting us, as we may not have the ambition, drive, or energy that we once had. Perhaps the regret is not doing more with our education to put us in a better place from a career standpoint. Perhaps we could have worked harder when we were younger. Or saved more money. It really doesn't matter what it was, here we stand, and the only question that beckons is; where do we go from here? Someone has recently said to me, "life is short, enjoy it." Another person said, "don't look back, look forward, and enjoy. What do we have left, 20 more years or so, max? So have fun!" This is all good advice and perspective.

I am working on changing my path and I can tell you that it is not the path of least resistance. I am working harder than I ever have, in an area where most of it is new to me. That is stressful and challenging as well. I am hoping the rewards and satisfaction of doing something awesome are worth the work and the risk. I'm sure it will be. If not, there is always plan B.

I was forced out of my stressful but stable and well-paying job. I experienced a medical set back. In and of themselves, each of these occurrences can be devastating. Combined, along with my desire to do something "more" with my life has led me to my new path. More details about that are forthcoming, so stay tuned.

So, if I could leave you with a take-a-way from this chapter, it would to be to understand that everyone has a fear, an insecurity, something that keeps them up at night, and they are probably dealing with something unpleasant, big or small. Whatever that unpleasant thing may be, it is important to them. With that understanding comes compassion. Compassion leads to caring. Caring leads to doing something that may comfort your friend or help make their life better. Just think, if we all had that type of understanding and compassion, what a better place this world would be.

CHAPTER 29

The Beginning of the New Beginning

So you know about the medical issues I faced in 2015, and I gave you a synopsis of life growing up, my college life, personal life, and work life, all of the good and bad. Let me now take you through the two years leading up to 2015.

I have been a very healthy person my entire life. Up until age 53 the last time I was in a hospital was to have my tonsils removed when I was 9. I would get the typical seasonal cold, but that was about it. I rarely missed school or work due to illness.

I will say I was remiss in getting an annual physical in my 30's and 40's, however I made it a point to go get this done once I turned 50. The customary colonoscopy was good, 7 years until I had to go back. The prostate was good. Blood pressure normal. Nothing to really worry about (I had no clue about the bad cholesterol).

At the age of 52, I really kicked up my workout regimen in the fall of 2013. My son Ryan was getting into power lifting and I wasn't about to let him get stronger than me. I did after all finally relinquish the household 100-yard dash title to him a few years earlier, so I had to hang on to some dignity.

In all seriousness, he motivated me to push myself in the gym as well as eat better. I have always been active, but as a golfer my workouts did not consist of heavy weight lifting. It is important to maintain flexibility in golf and the heavy lifting never seemed to work for me.

This time around however, I changed my goals from worrying about maintaining flexibility to building muscle. I have always been thin and saw the changes Ryan was making to his body in terms of size and strength, and thought it was time for me to build muscle as well.

It worked for the most part. I lifted heavier weights and added specific exercises that Ryan recommended to target certain muscle groups. I started in the fall of 2013 and by the spring of 2014 noticed the difference. I was filling out my shirts a bit better and felt a lot stronger.

When golf season came in 2014, I quickly discovered that the new found muscle didn't help my golf game. I lost some flexibility and with the stress of lifting weights and swinging a golf club came some new pain along with golfer's elbow. I still went to the gym but dialed it back quite a bit. I lowered the weight on most exercises and cut some out all-together, the ones that reduced my range of motion. It was during the workouts in late 2013 however, that I starting experiencing some odd symptoms.

I was an avid runner in high school and in college. I could run the mile under 5 minutes and did well when I ran track competitively. I would continue to run on and off after college and into my 40's. So, cutting out the heavy weights and trying to get into reasonably good shape with the inspiration supplied by my son, I attempted to run again. I started on the treadmill as the weather in Michigan in late fall, winter, and early spring makes it hard to run outside.

That is when I first noticed cramping in my right calf. At first I could run through it and it wasn't too terribly bad. I wrote it off to a muscle ache or thought maybe I am out of balance. I have heard about orthotics and have high arches and have experienced the joyful pain of plantar fasciitis, so I was sure that the cramping was caused by one of these things.

As spring of 2014 drew near, the cramping seemed to be getting worse. I could no longer run, but found that I could walk about 3 to 3.5 miles per hour on the treadmill. Anything more would lead to cramping.

After a month or so, my calf cramped up while walking at 3 miles per hour, and the time it took to cramp up became less and less. I could no longer walk for 20 minutes. 12 minutes was about the limit. After a couple of months, the time it took to cramp reduced down to just a few minutes, and I became more and more frustrated. Here I was, active and attempting to get into shape, and I can't even walk on the treadmill. Old age was creeping in, or so I thought.

Chuck, My Walk Through Life

With the arrival of spring of 2014, we were back on the golf course. I noticed it there too. I could hit a good drive close to 300 yards and by the end of the season, I was in severe pain walking to my tee shot. I found that if I stopped for a moment, the cramping would ease and I could trudge on another hundred yards or so. Typical of peripheral artery disease, but as I said earlier, that wasn't something that I knew even existed. I guess I am a knucklehead, but it really never dawned on me that it could be something serious. It got to the point where my right foot would get numb.

I did however mention it to my doctor at my annual physical that summer. He had me walk away from him and watched to see if my alignment was off, or if there was something he could see that was causing the cramping. There was nothing he could see that would be causing the problem so we kind of wrote it off. Big mistake.

CHAPTER 30

2 + 2 = 5

About that time, I had told my doctor that I was experiencing acid reflux symptoms. In retrospect it may have been another mistake to tell my doctor of my self-diagnosis, but to my defense, I did say I don't really know what acid reflux is, and that I didn't have the feeling in my throat or esophagus that I have read about. Maybe this would have led him to believe it was something else. Never did he or I put the two symptoms, leg cramps and tightness in the chest, together. Surely they were unrelated. Not so fast, mister! Anyways, I was prescribed an antacid and went on my merry way.

What I was experiencing was pressure in my chest, typically after a meal. Maybe I should change my diet? I recall one time on a hot day when I drank a lemonade and proceeded to mow the lawn. About halfway through my alleged acid reflux kicked in and I had to stop and sit down. For a brief moment I thought that I could be having a heart attack, it sure felt like it. Again, being in relatively good shape and health all my life I thought otherwise and the feeling subsided. Surely it was the acid in the lemonade, right?

As the summer turned to fall and during the last few weeks of our 9-hole golf league, I could no longer walk the course. It was too painful and most importantly it adversely affected my golf game. Now granted, I am 6'1" tall, 180 pounds, 34" waist, and I am relegated to a golf cart to play 9 holes on a flat golf course, while guys 60-80 pounds heavier than me, with presumable a 40+ inch waist are walking. I found that to be a bit embarrassing. Still, I didn't put 2 and 2 together successfully.

The fall and winter of 2014 came, I was back to the gym and the symptoms in my legs have progressed to where the cramping occurred almost instantly when attempting to walk on the treadmill. It was very frustrating to say the least. On the positive side, the antacids seemed to help. Which is ironic, because now I know that I didn't have acid reflux. I went back to lifting heavier weights and really never had any chest pain or shortness of breath. I do recall feeling a bit dizzy once or twice but it passed very quickly and I figured I was pushing a bit too hard.

CHAPTER 31

A Change of Plans

In my wife's family, Christmas was a time to gather and our house became the gathering place for the celebration for many years. It was passed on to my wife Kate and I when our family grew beyond the limits of what my in-laws home could accommodate. We were happy to do it. Then, as a matter of course, the next generation kept having kids and the family grew by leaps and bounds, totaling near 50 people, many of which are kids under the age of 10.

My father-in-law had passed in 2001, however it was extremely important to my mother-in-law that the Christmas gathering be held in our home. I had offered to have our golf club host it in their dining room. It was the perfect size for the kids to run around without me worryng about what was going to break next. I lost that battle (actually chose not to fight it) in 2013.

In 2014 our daughter Kim and her husband and four girls decided to come to Michigan, for Thanksgiving so they could spend Christmas at home. It had always been the other way around. We would go down there for Thanksgiving and they would come home for Christmas and the big family get together. Since they wouldn't be here for Christmas, talk began that maybe the big gathering (entire family) wouldn't happen. For one, it was hard to accommodate everyone, and without Kim and her family, maybe, just maybe, we could do something smaller where each family does their own thing. It was decided, and I will admit I was relieved that we were not hosting Christmas. I did feel a bit like the Grinch, but I was ready for something different.

Chuck, My Walk Through Life

Without the big gathering I asked Kate and Ryan if they would like to go somewhere for the holiday. I always figured it would be fun to spend the holiday away from home for some odd reason.

Being a huge Elvis fan, I suggested Memphis and Graceland, and believe it or not they agreed. I had hoped they agreed to this destination because of all that I have done in providing for the family, as well as my agreeing to go on vacations of their choosing for so many years. I still am not sure why they agreed to go to Memphis, since they often teased me about my affection for The King, but I really didn't care. I was excited.

As the time drew near, we noticed the weather in Memphis was not going to be good. We had talked about stopping in St. Louis on the way down, and had read that there were possibilities of terrorist threats there. Combine those two together and we decided to open it up for discussion. We still wanted to travel over the holiday, but weren't sure exactly where we would go. The only thing we knew was that we weren't going to fly anywhere due to the cost. It would have to be within driving distance.

Without too much hesitation, Ryan mentioned Washington D.C. I'm not sure why he suggested D.C., but we are both into history and the thought appealed to me. I checked the forecast and the weather was projected to be unseasonably warm, without rain. The decision was made. Washington D.C. it is. Was it a life-saving decision? Maybe.

Ryan's girlfriend at the time, Sara, came with us. She is a sweetheart and we always enjoyed her company. We stayed in a hotel about two miles or so away from the Lincoln Memorial. At first glance it looked like an easy walk. Driving was not an option as parking anywhere in D.C. is virtually impossible. We could take a scheduled tourist bus the next day, but it was too late to do so on our arrival date. Nevertheless, we wanted to check things out so we would have to hoof it.

It didn't take long to find out that my legs have not healed, as a matter of fact, they were worse. Far worse. I hadn't walked any significant distances in a couple of weeks and thought just maybe they would be better. I had no idea at the time it was an artery issue that, left unchecked, was only getting worse.

We walked about two blocks and the pain was severe. Ryan, being the ultimate tough guy told me to stop being such a baby and work through it. He used a different word that I won't repeat. I tried, it didn't work. I tried to explain to him how bad it was and after a while he seemed to understand.

Ryan and Sara would walk ahead and Kate would wait for me when I needed to stop. I pushed it as hard as I could, but it was bad and getting worse. I was stopping at every block to let the pain subside. It is hard to even bend your feet to walk when your calves are cramping so badly.

Back at the hotel, my wife said stop complaining and do something about it. It became apparent that I needed to check out on the internet what my problem could be. This was no ordinary muscle ache, it has been going on far too long, and I really don't think it is an alignment issue. I typed in the symptoms and as you already know, peripheral artery disease popped up. In reading the symptoms it was clear to me that was the problem, it described exactly how I was feeling.

Believing it was peripheral artery disease that was my issue, I still didn't have any clue how serious it would be. As a matter of fact, usually a good healthy eater, I ate a bar burger while on the DC trip, called the Burl Ives burger. It was a hamburger topped with a hot dog. I know, that was bad, really bad, and not my usual choice for food (loose interpretation). This particular pub didn't offer any healthy options, by the way, other than not eating, which would have been the smart thing to do.

We finished the trip and, not to pat myself on the back, I was a trooper. We walked a bunch and I trudged through it. Once back home, I called my doctor and you already know the rest of that story.

Pushing through the pain

CHAPTER 32

So now what?

So by now you know my story. I have had a pretty good life; healthy, successful in business to some extent, happy, and the ironic part is that I took care of myself pretty well. The artery issues have been mostly attributed to high genetic cholesterol. I wouldn't say I have been perfect all my life in terms of diet (Burl Ives burger, remember) or exercise, but of all the people I know, I would put myself in the top 25%. So why me? Why now?

I'm currently 55 years old, and eleven months removed from my last procedure. 2015 was a blur. Five procedures and countless trips to the doctor for testing, complications, and check-ups. In the end, I feel that my life was saved, I was lucky. What do you do with the second chance?

As I stated earlier, things happen in life. Not necessarily things that we want to happen, and some of these "things" can shake us to the core. Some can alter the path of your life, and you may not recognize it at the time, but can clearly see it happened when looking back. I can tell you that I have done a lot of looking back.

I never had any reason to consider my own mortality, but now after facing it, I have a lot of questions. This time, I want to create my own path knowing where that path is going to go and where it will end up. I want more control over where I am going and what I am going to do. None of us know when it will end. I'm not sure if that is good or bad, but it is what it is.

So what should I do? I mentioned to my cardiologist that I would like to do something. I wanted to get involved somehow, and help others who have gone through or are about to go through what I just did. I wanted to help people avoid heart disease. I just didn't know how. I did come to find out that the feeling of wanting to do something meaningful would only grow over time.

CHAPTER 33

Philosophy 101

During 2015 I continued to work. I would take a couple of days off, or work from home after each procedure for a day or two. I was lucky that my job allowed me the luxury to do that from time to time. When I did go to the office I was tired and less than enthused to be there. I did my job, and held things together for the most part. I was actually piecing together my best year ever from a financial standpoint. But something was missing.

After my third procedure in May, I called my boss and told him I was tired. He knew what I had been through and quite honestly, even though we disagreed about certain things at work from time to time, he couldn't have been more supportive. Ultimately, he told me to take a week off, forget about work, not to turn my computer on, and he would cover my team with the help of another manager while I was gone.

It helped from an energy standpoint. Ryan and I decided to drive down to Myrtle Beach, play golf and relax. It was a great week and I unplugged from work for the most part. But once back at work, I still had this feeling that selling wireless services and managing a sales team just wasn't satisfying.

After my medical experience, I thought there had to be something that I could sink my teeth into that would motivate me, and provide some sort of value to the greater good. I knew at age 54, I probably wasn't going to invent something that would make the world a better place. I knew that I single handedly couldn't solve world hunger or cure cancer, but surely there was something I could do. I kept thinking about it day after day.

CHAPTER 34

The Aha Moment

The last procedure that cleared out the blockage in my lower left leg in December of 2015, allowed me to walk much better than I had previously. The cardiologist told me to walk. Walk, walk, walk he said on more than one occasion, as have I in this book. He explained that it would help build bypass arteries in areas that may still be blocked, arteries that he couldn't get to. The words walk, walk, walk kept echoing in my head.

I made it a point to walk as much as I could. The winter of 2015-2016 was mild in Michigan. It allowed me to get outside and walk as opposed to relying on the treadmill. Our dog Roxy was a willing participant, accompanying me on virtually every trek around the half mile block.

Then on a weekday in the middle of winter, we were in for a major snow storm. Kate and Ryan were both at work and planning to be home at 6. I was already home. I called them with the idea to go to the local restaurant, Sugarbush, for dinner. I didn't feel like cooking. It is about three quarters of a mile from our house and I wanted to walk.

The snow was really coming down and both Ryan and Kate thought I was crazy for suggesting that we walk. They both said they would meet me at the restaurant on their way home as opposed to walking. I didn't argue, I could still walk and was looking forward to beating the elements. See, there is that competitive nature again.

It was blizzard-like conditions. I dressed warm; hat, gloves, boots, scarf, and put on sunglasses even though it was getting dark. I needed the sunglasses to keep the snow from blowing into my eyes. I was ready.

Chuck, My Walk Through Life

When I started out, a little voice inside my head said, just grab your car keys and drive, you idiot. It was tempting as the wind was howling and pushing the snow sideways. That voice was quickly silenced by my own determination and will. Call it drive or whatever you want, but I was dedicated to make this walk, albeit a short three quarter mile trek, a mile and a half roundtrip.

It felt great. The newly repaired leg was no longer in pain and I had no issue walking through the snow. It was actually quite pleasant. I figured I had to walk, and why let anything get in my way. I could walk through any storm especially for three quarters of a mile. If it was unbearable, I could ride home with Ryan or Kate.

It was quiet and serene. The snow was accumulating on the ground and branches of the trees that line Sugarbush Road; it was quite pretty, if you like snow. There wasn't much traffic and I was alone with my thoughts. Being in a good mood and still thinking about what I can do that would make my life more fulfilling, it then dawned on me. It came from out of the blue without warning or any conscious thought of the concept. I am going to walk across America.

Say again? Yep, walk across America. Sounds crazy right? It hit me and the more I thought about it the more excited I got. I like challenges and this would surely be the ultimate, at least for me. I had no regard for how I was going to do it, just the thought that I would do it. What a cool story it would make. Here is a guy that couldn't walk two city blocks, has coronary artery disease, and he is going to overcome all of that and walk across this great country of ours. The press would be interested, the heart community would love it (get it, heart and love), it could be a big deal. Perhaps I could do something meaningful after all.

By the time I arrived at the restaurant, Ryan and Kate were there already seated. I walked in, covered in snow, and they could see the excitement on my face, without knowing why I had this particular look. Maybe they figured I was smiling when I left the house, and it simple froze that way during the trek through the snow.

Kate immediately said, "Why do you have that look on your face?" She could tell something was up. She could always read me like a book. I told them I figured it out, I figured out how I can do something awesome. "I am going to walk across America," I said proudly.

They looked at each other and said, "Ok, sure you are". I could sense the disbelief in their voices. Picture the air coming out of a balloon and my face turning from a joyful look to the look of despair. Nope, I wasn't about to be deterred. I retained the joyful look and proudly said I was going to do this. They then realized I wasn't kidding and I proceeded win their confidence. The more I spoke about it, the more excited I became. Before we left, they knew I was serious and were starting to buy in.

I can tell you that I have been very conservative my whole life. Secure job, stable home, pay the bills on time, don't do anything to put your financial standing in jeopardy. I was leading a safe and boring life. The thought of doing anything crazy like this has never crossed my mind, ever.

This new thought gave me an epiphany moment that you only ever hear or read about. It truly excited me and gave life a new meaning. Time will tell how it will all work out, but for now I am pumped about the idea of doing something remarkable.

Just keep walking

CHAPTER 35

Life and Loss

Now that I hopefully have you as excited as I am about this upcoming challenge, I am going to ask you to hold the thought from the last chapter for a moment. This is the part of the book where we are going to get a bit more philosophical. We will touch on our emotions as human beings and maybe even a little on what it all means, as if anyone can really nail that one down.

I've written about events in our lives that I referred to as "curveballs". Something maybe that we didn't expect, as what happens to a hitter in baseball who is looking for the 90 mile an hour fastball, and gets a 76 mile an hour curveball that darts away from him. It can make you look foolish, frustrated, and throw you off your game, but only if you let it.

Life's curveballs can do the same thing. We may swing at, and miss the curveball, but how we respond after that is what is important. Everyone I know, has experienced some sort of loss. Some severe and life altering, and some more moderate. Regardless of the severity, the degree of which is very personal, what you choose to do next is what will determine your path and potential outcome.

I have seen it with many family and friends who have lost loved ones. These loved ones range from babies to elderly parents and grandparents, and everything in between. My best friend lost his 27-year old son in 2015. He was devastated as anyone would expect him to be. He chose to handle it with all the dignity and grace that could only be imagined. Although it hurts every day, he chose to continue with his life and be there for the other loved ones in his life, and live life in a way that makes us all proud to call him a friend.

Two of my brothers-in-law lost their wives in their early 50's to cancer. We have friends who have died of pancreatic cancer in their early 50's. Friends I know have lost parents, brothers, sisters and kids. The older we get the more funerals we attend. With it, I have seen all sorts of ways to cope and handle these difficult situations.

I personally lost a friend/co-worker who committed suicide in his late 20's. That was hard, as it seemed so senseless. I lost a step-granddaughter that I never got to know, but who will always be in our hearts. Molly died shortly after birth. Two years later, Lyla came along. Not necessarily to fill the void, but to prove again that life goes on no matter how devastating the loss can be.

Life does go on, not for the deceased of course, at least not in the physical world of earth, but for the survivors. It can be difficult at times depending on the relationship that existed with the deceased. People that experience a medical diagnosis that rocks their world, like cancer or heart disease, also have to adapt, and they typically do, somehow.

Adapt is the key word. Our minds might take us to places we don't really want to go, and consume our thoughts. In my experience, and believe me, my mind has a mind of its own if that makes any sense, I found that analyzing the situation on paper, spelling out and creating options for moving forward in writing, actually helped. Then, with this logic in black and white, I could choose the best option. This was the best way to put my mind's mind at ease. This may not work in every situation, but at some point, information and logic should come into play when dealing with any loss, and help balance out the emotional component of it all.

You have to find the best way for you to deal with your particular situation. You can get input from all sorts of people that will tell you how they think you should move forward, and it is not wrong to listen. I listened to as much advice as people were willing to give. You never know when you are going to get the advice that makes perfect sense for your situation. However, in the end, you have to be at ease with your choices and or path, and you have to buy in and be 100% committed.

My plan was to get healthy and make sure that my heart disease wouldn't continue to control my quality of life. I wanted to continue to lead an active lifestyle as I have my entire life, without restrictions. I set goals for daily exercise, and made sure my diet was as heart healthy as possible.

I ultimately set the goal of goals for me, walking across America. It will be something I will have to be completely committed to, and measure my progress on a daily basis, right up until the event.

My point here, is that after a "curveball" you need to stay busy and stay committed. Keep your mind occupied. Do the things that inspire you or make you feel good. Nobody lives forever, so why waste the time we each have on this earth. No bad days! That is a slogan that I frequently remind myself of when my mind starts going the wrong direction. I saw that on a bumper of a car. No bad days! There is so much beauty in the world to behold. There are so many of the little joys that shouldn't be taken for granted.

No matter your situation, if you are still alive and breathing, you can choose how you want to feel. Remember, no bad days!

CHAPTER 36

More Philosophy and Stuff

Let's do an exercise. Write down the 5 things you think life is. It's easy and I will give you some ideas. Life is:

Challenging
Unpredictable
A jig saw puzzle
Meant to be enjoyed
Complex

You get the idea. Now jot down your 5 items before reading any further. Imagine a certain game show music playing here...

Great! Now, list 5 things you are grateful for. I will help here as well. I am grateful for:

My family
My health
My friends
Freedom
The fact that someone invented golf and baseball

Think of those things and think about how it made you feel. That is pretty cool stuff and stuff that we sometimes take for granted, right?

Last step. Now that you are in a grateful mindset, list 5 things that you think life is again.

Life is... did your list change? Mine did. It changed because your perspective on life changed after realizing what you were grateful for. If it didn't change, maybe you have a good handle on your emotions and on life in general, and don't take too many things for granted. That's great.

If it did change, keep reminding yourself daily of what is good in your life and hold on to those feelings. Life isn't meant to be easy. Think about the people hundreds or thousands of years ago and how they had to survive the elements without proper shelter, disease without good medical attention, war without protection, etc., etc., etc.

But life can be easier in our own minds if we have the right perspective. I have struggled with this many times in my life, not realizing what is truly important or how lucky I have been. It is all perspective. Even being diagnosed with coronary artery disease at the age of 53, I am an extremely lucky man for all that life has given me.

We all don't have to look too far to find those that have it worse off than us. That's not it, though. We don't have to look too far to find those that are better off than us. But are they really? Do they know it? Do you know if they know it? Better off how? One of the happiest people I ever knew didn't have two nickels to rub together (a younger me), so money isn't a good barometer. So then what is?

What is important is that we appreciate our own lives and how they are comprised. It is not about measuring yourself against anyone else in terms of money, the size of the house, or job status, or stature in the community. It is about being happy. Happy that we are alive. Happy that the sun comes up each and every day. Happy for a million other reasons. All we have to do is let it happen.

If you need reminders, then post them on your mirror, so you can see them every day. Send yourself a text with a happy thought or something to be grateful for. Call someone and tell them you love them. There are a million ways to improve your mood. It starts with the heart! Do more things from the heart, and you will be a happier person. I believe that completely as it's happened to me, and the beauty is you don't have to wait for a catastrophic event.

Chapter 37

Stop Trying to Keep Up with The Joneses

Now that we might have a better idea on what makes life worth living, what defines you is a question you have to ask of yourself. For a long time, I thought it was the number on my W2 at the end of the year, or how much I had in my 401k. We work 40 to 80 hours a week and dive into our jobs with all of our being, so the dollar amount generated is really reflective of your success right? Well…

When people meet, one of the first questions is "what do you do?" That is what defines you, right? It has to be prestigious to make you feel of value, right? What you do for a living and how it is perceived by others is what defines you, isn't it? Maybe, but maybe not. My feeling is that it depends what you do, and here is the important part; whether or not it fulfills and thrills you, and how it possibly impacts the lives of others.

Let's face it, not all of us are on a path to cure cancer, end hunger, uncover the meaning of life, or find a way to end war and fighting in this world. Just because we aren't doing those things, doesn't mean we aren't doing something meaningful, which may be impacting the lives of others, directly or indirectly.

I have managed people for most of my career, and although it can be said that all we really did was sell communication services, I have found meaning or value in the fact that I helped those I worked with to meet some of their personal and professional goals. We also helped customers overcome significant business challenges. Heck, maybe some of those customers were working on a cure for cancer or attempting to solve world hunger (actually, some were).

Somewhere in all of this I found that there is far more to it, and although I seemingly knew that before, my financial success is what woke me up every day to go to work and make a living. I had to provide for my family and I found a career that did just that. But was it enough? Did it thrill me or was I just going through the motions? Was I a meaningful specific in this world or just a wandering generality?

Yes, there is more to it than money. Sure, everyone likes money and prestige. Everyone would love to say they are a Brain Surgeon or a Rocket Scientist. But is how others perceive you really what defines you? Only if you let it.

So is it what you do that is important? Is it how much money you make? Is it how others perceive what you do, and the more impressed they are, the more meaningful you are?

When you really get to the core of all of this, it really isn't any of these things unless you think it is. In other words, it is how you feel about yourself that is important. Have you lived up to your own expectations? Are you happy with you?

Isn't having a loving family more important than any job you might have? Isn't being a happy person no matter what your lot in life is, more important than most anything else?

The value you put on these things is what is important. My brush with my own mortality helped remind me of such. You define you. You set the criteria, and you measure yourself. Only you can make you happy, so get the heck out of the way of being happy.

I had a good job for the most part, one that provided a solid living for my family. I have a great family, wonderful kids and grandkids, a nice house, a nice car. Am I defined? Am I happy? Family yes, job and stuff, nah, that's not it.

The feeling that I am doing what I was meant to do, that I am striving to meet my own potential, that I can help others and be that footnote in this world, that is what will ultimately help define me. That was the missing piece. The family was always there. The internal happiness is up to me.

When I tell people that I am going to walk across America, some think I'm crazy. I know that, I can tell by the look on their face, or the immediate Forrest Gump reference. That is approximately 10% of the time or so. Heck, my wife and son initially thought I had a screw loose when I told them. However, the vast majority have said things like "you are my hero", "I admire you for what you are about to do", "I am proud to call you a friend". Those are the things that define you. Thanks Dave, Jennifer and Patrick.

If you haven't put it together yet, I will be as straightforward as I can be. You are defined for the type of person that you are. From that comes the self-respect, the loving family, happiness (key ingredient), the friends, success in however you want to measure it, and the respect from others. If you are a religious person, it comes from knowing that your maker is proud and approves of you. What more is there? That your parents approve and are proud. That your kids are proud of you and love you no matter how much money you make. That is the true "it".

CHAPTER 38

My "It"

For some reason, I felt that creating an organization that helps people with heart disease is what I am supposed to do at this stage in my life. I'm not exactly sure why, but it seems right and I am moving forward in that direction. Part of that responsibility is taking on the enormous challenge of walking across the country. That is my "it". Something I can look back and say, I did that, and hopefully it inspired others to overcome whatever has challenged them. At this stage in the game I have no idea what the outcome is going to be, but then again, who really does?

After we came up with this idea, we spent the next few days talking about it and the ideas were flowing like Niagara Falls. They just kept coming. We could do some great things with this. Surely, a guy who couldn't walk 100 yards at a time, that is now going to walk 3,000+ miles would be a big deal. We could do this to benefit others. Once we thought about it in that light, the ideas came even faster.

We have created a nonprofit, Walk For The Beat, and are working on ideas for promoting the cross country walk, along with raising funds. We have the support of hundreds of people thus far. We even bought an RV and are going to sell our house next year. Talk about commitment. Talk about changing the status quo. Talk about crazy...the old Chuck would have never even considered this. The new Chuck, although a bit scared about how it will all turn out, is moving forward, 100% committed.

We are planning to send the message to America's youth by demonstrating CPR techniques as we walk across the country as well as providing seminars on living a heart healthy lifestyle, both through fitness and nutrition. I am currently working with many people in those related fields, and I am not going to stop there. There is so much work to be done.

Additionally, if we are able to accomplish our goals, we will provide support to youth athletic leagues. It truly starts with the younger generation. Get them on the path of healthy, active living. That is the key.

Our mission is simple, create a movement that attacks the causes of cardiovascular disease. Our vision is even more simple, a world with fewer catastrophic cardiovascular related events.

Along with working with America's youth, if all goes well, we plan to provide financial support for heart research, and to those in need who may have experienced a catastrophic cardiovascular heart related event. We have big plans. Our organization as I mentioned above, but will shamelessly plug again, is called Walk for The Beat.

If this all works out and I am able to physically pull this off, perhaps I will have found my "it". The thing that makes me tick. It has already provided me with energy and ambition that I haven't known for years.

I have spent the better part of the past 30 years working for a buck, funding our retirement and fighting rush hour traffic twice a day. Now, I would embark on a path that has none of that (well, probably some traffic along the way). My future is uncertain, as is my financial situation. However, if we can pull it off, it could benefit many, many people. Maybe there is even hope for me becoming a footnote in the history of this world, although that's not what's really important, it is truly about how we can impact the lives of others.

My point here is that you never really know when it will happen, but you do have the ability to overcome the odds, and change the path your life is currently on, if, and this is a big if, you are not satisfied with your life's current path. It might be a simple or a complex challenge, but it will all start with a straight forward yes or no decision to move in a new direction, or to maintain the status quo, and then a commitment to the extent that you may not have experienced before.

Everyone has to make their own decision and status quo might be right for some people. Everyone has different circumstances and tolerance to risk. A lot of things need to be considered. For me, it became easier when my job ended in June. I could now focus all my attention on our new passion. Plus, Ryan turned 24 in July and is ready to venture out on his own. After 30 some years, it will finally be just Kate and I (oh and Roxy,

Chuck, My Walk Through Life

who is technically Ryan's dog. No the dog isn't going with us on the cross country walk, LOL, as much as I will miss her).

Kate has been 100% behind this crazy idea, and is really looking forward to the trip. It should keep us busy for 8 months or so. Our plan is to start at the Pacific Ocean in Oceanside California on October 1st of 2017, and walk to the Atlantic Ocean, beach to beach, to North Myrtle Beach, South Carolina.

You will be able to follow us on Facebook, Twitter, and on our website at www.walkforthebeat.org, and I personally invite you to do so. It will be the adventure of a lifetime for us, and we will be sharing as much as we can for the world to see, with the hopes that our vision of reducing catastrophic cardiovascular events is realized.

CHAPTER 39

Closing Comments

Looking back on life is interesting. It may even be a bit dangerous and disconcerting. We are where we are in life and we are here primarily because this is the path we either chose or allowed to be chosen for us. I would guess that virtually everyone has a regret or two, but guess what, it is what it is.

We are here at our respective places in life, and that cannot be changed. What can change is where we go from here. The old "begin with the end in mind" fits in nicely here. When it is all said and done, and we are ready to take our last breaths, how do we want our life story to read? Regardless of what has transpired in our lives, we have the ability today, to begin to write how it will all play out and how our stories will read.

It all starts with determining what it is we want out of life. Finding our "it" is a good place to start. Finding what thrills and excites us. It could be anything really. You might want to be known as a great business person. That's fine, start a business if you haven't already. Take a class to further your learning. Find a mentor. There are a lot of ways to improve your business acumen. You may want to be known as the best mother or father in the world. If that is the case, then go buy a t-shirt that says so, just kidding. But you could stop and determine how you are currently raising your kids, and if every decision and every interaction is helping you achieve that number one status, and truly doing what is right for your child's development.

Chuck, My Walk Through Life

It may sound easier that it really is. I will say that making the decision really isn't that hard. Lay it out, think it through, then decide. Once you decide to chase a dream, make a career change, or whatever your "it" is, it is then the commitment and the work afterwards that will be challenging. As they say, nothing worthwhile ever comes easy.

In my situation I will be taking almost two years out of my life to chase a dream at age 55, without knowing where my next pay check will be coming from. I have saved some money, although not enough to be fully retired, but enough to get by during these two years. Social security money won't be available for seven more years so at some point I will have to figure out how to earn an income again. But that isn't my purpose. Dying with a ton of money in the bank isn't what it's all about, right? Sorry kids, but if there is any money left over when I die, I miscalculated, LOL. It is about experiencing life.

On our walk across America, I want to meet as many people as we can possibly meet. I want to talk about how they can avoid heart disease. We want to teach America's youth about CPR and heart healthy fitness and diet tips. There is so much good that we can do. America has become obese and it is killing us, literally. We can start to make a dent in that trend and work to reverse it. That is what I decided to focus on for the next however many years. So, in terms of beginning with the end in mind, when I have taken my last breath, and someone says the name Chuck Woolaver, people will say, that guy overcame a lot, conquered a tremendous challenge, and really did a lot for America in terms of advancing heart healthy living. If that happens, I will have become a meaningful specific in this world.

Here is my challenge to you, how do you want your final story to read? What do you want to be known for? Do you want to be the guy who worked until he was 70, retired, and was told he has 6 months to live shortly thereafter? I know someone who is currently in that boat. Do you want fame? Do you want to help others? Do you want to provide the best possible inheritance for your kids? All of those are ok. Figure it out and plan to make it happen. It is all possible once you do.

CHAPTER 40

Closing Comments…Really

So there you have it. My life in a nutshell and where I am going from here. I hope you enjoyed the book. I do have some tips for any and all who may be interested. They are as follows:

1) Find your "it". What thrills you and excites you.
2) Don't be averse to taking chances in order to achieve your goals.
3) Keep the big picture in mind. None of us get out of here alive, so go for it when you can.
4) Value what should be valued, and eliminate the crap (philosophical term).
5) Follow your heart and be happy.

From a medical perspective:

1) Pay attention to your symptoms.
2) Research so you can understand the discussions and treatment options.
3) Be your own advocate.
4) Doctors, as much as they try, aren't always right, question them.

My best to all of you, and I sincerely hope that you find everything you want in life. Make it worth living and do it with passion and excitement. It starts with the heart!

Printed in the United States
By Bookmasters